THE GOOD COOK BOOK BY YVES

This book is lovingly dedicated, to my wife, Sylvia, and my two children, Ariane and Marcus.

Library of Congress Cataloging-in-Publication Data.
Potvin, Yves.
The Good Cook Book by Yves / Yves Potvin
ISBN: 0-9684817-1-X
Printed in Canada
Second Edition

1 2 3 4 5 6 7 8 9 10

www.yvesveggie.com

CONTENTS

ENTRÉES

ACKNOWLEDGEMENTS

First I would like to thank Vesanto Melina, R.D., and Chef Joseph Forest for helping me put this cookbook together. They have been a very important part in making this cookbook a reality and working with them was a delightful experience. A special thanks to Chef Jozsef Bogdan, François Gagnon and Olivier Andretti for helping to create some of these wonderful recipes.

Yves Veggie Cuisine was founded 15 years ago and I have a great deal of appreciation for the many people who have contributed to the success of this company.

Special thank-yous to: My brother Claude, and my sister Francine for believing in me and lending some of the capital needed to start this company. My parents for raising me in an environment that taught me to always strive to surpass myself and allowing me to dream. My sister Lucie for her continuous encouragement and to my brother Jean-Paul for showing me, in his own way, how precious life is. Richard Gagné and Jean Coté for being there at the right time and in the right place. Michael Weiner who taught me a lot about the industry and Henk Hoogenkamp for his continued support. Lucie Bellefeuille for suggesting that I should become a chef and to Jacques Hébert who directed me towards healthy cooking. Omar Flamenco, Carlos Palomo and Hien Trinh, for their part in building the foundation of this company. Ron Trepanier and Laurie Jones, Clare Thomson and Don Daintrey for their passion and their commitment. My assistant Tracy Wright for helping me organize my life and for pulling the cookbook together.

And last but not least, to my great friend Ken Bolton, a special thanks for being who you are and for helping me bring this company to where it is today.

ALL ABOUT YVES

YVES POTVIN

And so, you ask, who is Yves? Let me tell you a little bit about myself, and the company Yves Veggie Cuisine.

As you may have already guessed, I'm French. So my interest in good food comes naturally. My mother is an excellent cook. When I was a child, my home was always filled with the aroma of something delicious cooking. I saw that it took my mother a great deal of time in the kitchen, to satisfy the different eating preferences of a large family. As I grew up, I enjoyed taking part in simple summer barbecues and came to appreciate the more sophisticated foods of my French heritage.

My love of great food, and perhaps the inspiration of my mother, led me to work as a chef, creating classical cuisine and food to delight the palate. As I began to work in upscale dining establishments, I noticed in restaurant clientele and in myself an emerging interest in health, fitness and good nutrition. As I experimented with new recipes, I discovered that eating light, healthy foods left me alert, refreshed, full of energy and truly nourished.

My new-found energy inspired me to take a journey that changed my life. In 1983, I cycled across the North American continent in just under two months. As I traveled, I could see that the favorite foods of North Americans – burgers, hot dogs, even sandwich slices – deliver a freedom people love, but not the nutrition they deserve. I became fascinated with a desire to balance health and nutrition with simplicity and good taste.

As I cycled, the questions came. Could easy-to-use products be created without the features that people dislike – preservatives, saturated fat, and cholesterol? Could healthier versions of favorite foods meet and even exceed our standards of flavor? These questions interested and inspired me. I didn't know it then, but my life's purpose had begun.

And then it hit me.

As crazy as the idea seemed, it became clear that I wanted to create a new hot dog. It would be the same shape and the same flavor as the traditional hot dog I loved as a child, but it would be made of ingredients from plant foods. Above all, it would taste good and be good for people!

I had the idea. Then the work began. I became a one-man operation, obsessed with creating the perfect tasting Veggie Dog. The hard work paid off. When Yves Veggie Wieners reached the marketplace, they struck a chord with consumers. People were hungry for healthy alternatives to conventional fast foods. They literally ate up Yves Veggie Wieners. From that point our operation grew very quickly.

Today, Yves Veggie Cuisine is the accomplishment of a team of creative and dedicated experts. Together, we produce a full line of tasty, convenient, fat-free, cholesterol-free products. We're constantly branching out and looking for new ways to help people enjoy healthy, delicious meals. We recognized that for a lot of people, healthy eating means making some dietary changes and learning new recipes. We knew the time for a cook book, with healthy, delicious, easy-to-prepare recipes, was right. Voilà…here you have *The Good Cook Book by Yves*. Good food for a good life.

YVES GRILLING HIS FAVORITE
SUMMER '65

TRADITIONAL RECIPES WITH A DIFFERENCE

Everywhere you look these days, you see healthy changes in the products filling many supermarket carts. But that's not all. Our taste in recipes is also changing. In *The Good Cook Book by Yves,* we offer traditional recipes that your family has enjoyed together over the years – with a difference.

Twenty years ago, it was common for a Stroganoff recipe to begin with 1/4 cup of butter. Back then, cookbooks didn't show a nutritional analysis beneath each recipe, but we know that way of eating sure piled on the pounds! If there had been a nutritional analysis, it would have shown that 75 percent of the calories were from fat.

Here at Yves Veggie Cuisine, our team of chefs has cut down on much of the butter, oil, and sour cream, while still maintaining the delightful flavor of our favorite dishes.

A FEW WORDS ON FAT

I'd like to say a few more words about fat. I've always found that it's easier to add fat to a recipe, than to remove fat from high-fat ingredients. So, when you use Yves Veggie Cuisine, you have a great deal of freedom.

If you want low fat eating, you can closely follow the recipes in this book, since our products are fat-free to begin with. Alternatively, you may like to cook with a small quantity of good quality olive or canola oil. Some of our recipes show a range in the amount of oil you may want to use.

It's your choice. All of the recipes in *The Good Cook Book by Yves* can be adjusted to your own preference.

REMEMBER WHAT REALLY MATTERS

In closing, I think of my father, now in his seventies, who has a growing appreciation for what really matters in life. He has come to realize that whatever money or material goods you have, there is nothing so valuable as your health. Our good health touches every aspect of our lives – mental, emotional, even spiritual. When we eat better, we feel better. And when we feel good about ourselves, we feel better about everyone around us.

I believe we all have a special place in this world and everyone has a chance to change the world in some way. It is a privilege to make a small contribution with food that is healthy, good for the world and appreciated by so many people.

I leave you now with *The Good Cook Book by Yves,* and the hope that it enriches your diet and your life.

Bon appétit!

Yves Potvin
Founder and President of Yves Veggie Cuisine
VANCOUVER, CANADA

Good food for life!

SOY IS HEART HEALTHY

On October 20, 1999, after extensive research and clinical trials,
the United States Food and Drug Administration recognized the importance
of soy's cholesterol-lowering effects, and claimed that:

*"Diets low in saturated fat & cholesterol that
include 25 grams of soy protein may reduce the risk of heart disease "*

APPROVED FDA PRODUCT CLAIM. ALL YVES PRODUCTS, EXCEPT FOR ENTRÉES & TOFU WIENERS,
CONTAIN AT LEAST 6.25 GRAMS OF SOY PROTEIN PER SERVING.

YVES TAKES GREAT TASTE TO HEART

At Yves Veggie Cuisine, soy has always been the main source of protein
in everything we make. Low in fat and cholesterol, with an average of
7g of soy protein per serving, Yves Veggie Cuisine products are a delicious
way to enjoy the benefits of soy. And we do mean delicious. After all, no
matter how good soy is for you, you won't eat it if it doesn't taste great.
It's easy to add a little soy to your diet and never compromise on quality
or taste when you choose from dozens of Yves Veggie Cuisine products.

THE HEALTHY BENEFITS OF SOY

Best of all it tastes great!

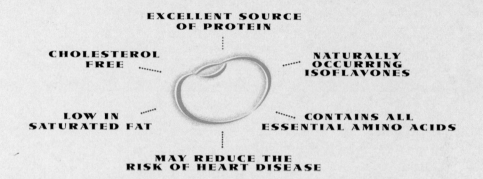

EXCELLENT SOURCE
OF PROTEIN

CHOLESTEROL
FREE

NATURALLY
OCCURRING
ISOFLAVONES

LOW IN
SATURATED FAT

CONTAINS ALL
ESSENTIAL AMINO ACIDS

MAY REDUCE THE
RISK OF HEART DISEASE

SOY: THE NEW SUPER FOOD?

With recent FDA claims about soy's ability to reduce heart disease, its proven ability to reduce cholesterol, and its powerful protein content, there's no doubt that this humble bean has earned its Super-Food title. However, while soy may be making news in America, it's definitely not new. The health benefits of soy have been known and enjoyed by Eastern cultures for centuries. And in the more recent past, we discovered the joy of soy, and made it the base of the Yves Veggie Cuisine product line. Soybean products have now become a popular alternative to meat, eggs and dairy products. When we look at all its benefits, it's easy to understand why soy is super.

OUR FAMILY OF PRODUCTS

VEGGIE DOGS

VEGGIE BURGERS

VEGGIE SLICES

VEGGIE GROUND ROUND

VEGGIE ENTRÉES

Over the next few pages, we'd like to introduce you to Yves Veggie Cuisine's family of products, and provide tips for cooking in this new, healthy way. We'll demystify a few French cooking terms and list kitchen tools that will help you cook with ease. We give a little background for the nutritional analysis that accompanies each recipe. For label readers, we shed light on two concepts that can be confusing: 'grams of fat' and 'percent calories from fat'. Yves products and our recipes have been created with your health in mind and with good nutrition as a key ingredient. We hope you and your family will enjoy these new, improved versions of traditional favorites.

Yves Veggie Cuisine's family of products includes food from five categories:

YVES VEGGIE DOGS include Tofu Wieners, Veggie Wieners, Jumbo Veggie Dogs, Hot and Spicy Jumbo Veggie Dogs, Veggie Chili Dogs and Veggie Breakfast Links.

YVES VEGGIE BURGERS include Veggie Burger Burgers, Garden Vegetable Patties and Black Bean and Mushroom Burgers.

YVES VEGGIE SLICES include Veggie Pepperoni, Veggie Pizza Pepperoni, Canadian Veggie Bacon, Veggie Turkey, Ham and Deli Slices.

YVES VEGGIE GROUND ROUND comes in two varieties – Original and Italian.

YVES VEGGIE ENTRÉES include a growing number of 'heat and serve' entrées including Veggie Chili, Veggie Country Stew and Pasta Entrées.

There are two important features to remember when handling our products:

Yves Veggie Cuisine products are precooked and ready to eat.

Yves products look like meat and taste like meat, but they should be cooked a little differently – more quickly.

Heating many of Yves products will accentuate your eating enjoyment, however they don't need the long cooking times that many traditional dishes require. This is an enormous benefit of using Yves Veggie Cuisine products. In recent years, issues of food safety have dictated that meats be cooked thoroughly, and even overcooked. This is not necessary with Yves Veggie Cuisine. Yves products are created from soy protein in a scrupulously hygienic environment; they are precooked and are much lower in fat than meat. For best results, take care not to overcook Yves Veggie Cuisine products. Packages give specific instructions and times for heating, steaming, frying or microwaving the various items.

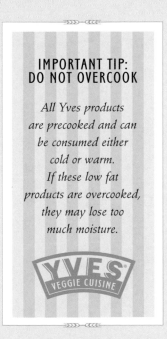

**IMPORTANT TIP:
DO NOT OVERCOOK**

All Yves products are precooked and can be consumed either cold or warm. If these low fat products are overcooked, they may lose too much moisture.

Yves Veggie Ground Round

This versatile product replaces ground beef in recipes. However for Shepherd's Pie, Cabbage Rolls or Bolognese Sauce, instead of sautéeing the product in oil and then cooking it for a long period of time, add Yves Veggie Ground Round midway or at the end of the cooking process. It simply requires heating.

*New easy to open package!
Simply snip edge & tear to
release link.*

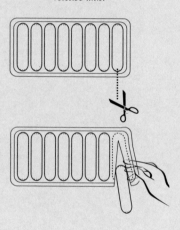

Yves Veggie Ground Round absorbs some of the water present in a sauce, so if you are reheating a dish the following day, add a bit of liquid to thin the sauce.

Yves Veggie Burgers and Patties

Yves burgers do not have to be fried, grilled, barbecued or microwaved 'til they're well done. Just cook until they are heated through, and they're ready-to-eat. In recipes such as Stroganoff, Vegetable Curry or Hungarian Goulash, a sauce is created first, then Yves burgers are added.

Yves Veggie Wieners, Dogs and Links

Here's a trick to retain the juiciness in your low fat Yves wieners and dogs. Steam them! Steam or simmer wieners for three minutes or until heated through. To heat by microwave, place Yves wieners in a microsafe dish, cover with water, loosely cover dish with a lid or plastic wrap, and microwave on high power for 2–3 minutes. Yves wieners may also be barbecued, roasted, baked and grilled, however avoid over-cooking because it gives a drier product.

For ease in removing fresh Yves Veggie Breakfast Links from their packaging, cut film parallel to links at one end, as shown in the diagram. Then, peel the flat surface of the film, releasing the link. Steam, as with wieners, or fry in a little oil until heated through, and enjoy!

Yves Veggie Slices

Yves slices are all ready-to-eat without any cooking. However the authentic flavor of Yves Canadian Veggie Bacon comes through best if it is briefly sautéed in a small amount of oil. Avoid overcooking Yves Veggie Pepperoni and other Yves slices, whether they are on top of a pizza or in a frying pan. On pizzas, you may cover Yves slices with a little tomato sauce, to retain their moisture.

Yves Fresh, Ready-to-Heat Entrées

Yves currently offers five delicious entrées made with Yves' award-winning Veggie Ground Round. Yves entrées are designed to be ready in approximately three minutes, using the stove top or a microwave. Simply follow the package directions for a fast, delicious, nutritious meal.

Pasta fans will love Yves three pastas: Veggie Penne, Macaroni and Lasagna with their hearty mixture of noodles smothered in a rich tomato sauce and fine herbs.

Yves Veggie Chili is made with Veggie Ground Round and whole red kidney beans and can be stretched to serve more people or a bigger appetite with additional ingredients such as corn, chopped peppers and Yves Veggie Wieners. You may also add fresh herbs, such as cilantro. Yves Veggie Chili can be the base for a soup such as Mexican Bean Soup, by adding soup stock, salsa and a touch of lime or try Yves Veggie Country Stew which is full of veggie meatballs and fresh vegetables simmered together in a delicious gravy.

SAFE HANDLING OF YVES PRODUCTS

With Yves Veggie Cuisine, you've brought home a super-healthy product. Here are some tips to help you look after these top quality foods.

Q. **How do I handle and store Yves Veggie Cuisine Veggie Ground Round, Wieners, Slices and Burgers?**

A. Yves Veggie Cuisine should be handled with the same care as other perishable foods. As soon as possible after purchase, place Yves Veggie Ground Round, Wieners, Slices and Burgers in a refrigerator or freezer.

Q. **How do I store Yves Veggie Cuisine entrées?**

A. Yves entrées such as Yves Veggie Chili, Veggie Country Stew, Macaroni and Penne maintain their quality best when they are refrigerated, rather than frozen.

Q. **How long can I store Yves products in my refrigerator or freezer?**

A. Products that have not been opened should be consumed by the 'best before' date, which is stamped on the back of every package.

Q. **Once I have opened a package of Yves Veggie Ground Round, Wieners, Slices or Burgers, how long may I store any unused product?**

A. Once a package has been opened, the product may be covered in plastic wrap, refrigerated and used within 5 to 6 days.

Q. **How do I thaw Yves products after they have been frozen?**

A. Thaw Yves products in your refrigerator.

Q. **Can Yves products be re-frozen?**

A. No, for best quality it is recommended that you do not re-freeze Yves products that have been previously frozen and then thawed.

COOKING TECHNIQUES & TERMS

Are you intimidated by cooking terms? Many of these terms come from the French language, but in fact the skills are not so difficult. For terms in this book, here's what we mean:

BLANCH: Cook partially or briefly in boiling water. Blanching brightens colors in vegetables and loosens skins of fruits and almonds.

STEAM: Place in direct contact with steam. For example, place Veggie Wieners in a basket steamer in a pot, above a small amount of water. Bring water to a boil. Steaming retains the juiciness and plumpness of Veggie Wieners and the nutritional value of foods.

JULIENNE: Cut 'matchstick thin'.

DICE: Cut into pieces no larger than the fingernail on your small finger.

MINCE: Cut into a very small dice. Mincing creates as much surface area as possible, allowing flavor to disperse into the prepared dish.

CHOP: Cut roughly into irregular sized pieces.

SAUTÉ: Cook quickly, over medium to high heat, moving cooked food to the edge of the pan. When you use a light skillet with tilting sides, food may be moved by tossing the cooked food to the edges of the skillet, with a flick of the wrist. You may also use a pancake flipper or spoon.

GOLDEN RULES FOR EASY COOKING

1. **Invest in proper kitchen equipment.**
   A few pieces of good quality equipment will contribute joy to your meal preparation, with healthy eating as an end result. (See pages 16–17.)

2. **Read recipe at least twice before you begin.**
   This familiarizes you with the ingredients needed, preparation techniques and sequence of steps.

3. **Gather all ingredients before you start cooking.**
   Before you begin, gather all the ingredients on the counter. Few events are as frustrating as discovering, near the completion of a recipe, that you are missing a crucial ingredient.

4. **Learn to make a few things well.**
   Choose a few recipes and make them several times until you feel confident. When you have mastered these, you'll have confidence to introduce innovations, if you wish, varying ingredients to create new dishes.

5. **Simplify the amount of food served per meal.**
   Recipes in this book are simple but nutritious. For a nourishing and filling meal, only one or two items are needed. For instance, soup can be served with hearty bread or multigrain rolls, entrées with rice or noodles and salad with a soy beverage.

6. **Stock your pantry with convenience foods.**
   Convenience foods such as canned beans, pasta noodles and, of course, Yves Veggie Cuisine products, will considerably reduce meal time.

7. **Prepare some ingredients in advance.**
   If time is at a premium, prepare in advance a supply of salad, cooked rice or beans that will last for several meals. Salad keeps well in tightly sealed containers. Later in the week, rice may be used for Cabbage Rolls. Portions of beans may be frozen for future batches of Baked Beans with Veggie Wieners or Veggie Mexi Mix. Double or triple the recipe for Veggie Meatballs and freeze them for quick pasta meals.

8. **Get help in the kitchen.**
   Benefit from the tendency of family members to wander by the kitchen before mealtime by inviting their help. Children learn to love vegetables through the sociable and sensory experience of helping prepare dinner. With time, youngsters can create an entire meal with minimal supervision. Later on, they will appreciate leaving home equipped with some kitchen sense.

9. **Take a cooking course.**
   Learn to chop vegetables, handle a knife and develop kitchen confidence to last a lifetime. Adult education programs, cookware shops and some cookbook stores offer classes.

10. **Trust your intuition.**
    The process of cooking is not just a matter of logic; it involves all five senses, plus intuition. When you wonder "Is it time to add the spices?" or "I wonder if the noodles are cooked?" use all your awareness, outer and inner. Slowing down to listen and sense may the greatest contribution to your health. Most of all, have fun, be creative – and discover the joys of cooking.

Yves Veggie Cuisine products are convenient and can be prepared with a minimum of equipment. Investing in a few good kitchen tools will give excellent returns to health and pleasure. Here are the basics:

1. **Chef Knife and Steel**

   The single item that will most increase your enjoyment and efficiency in the kitchen is an 8" chef knife that holds its edge, stays sharp, and feels good in your hand. Keep its edge with a German steel or knife sharpener, and occasionally have the knife sharpened at a kitchen supply shop. When you use it, take care!

2. **Cutting Board**

   Your cutting board is your workspace, so allow ample room to chop and prepare ingredients. The minimum is an easily cleaned 8 x 12" plastic board. If you have plenty of counter space, treat yourself to a 13 x 20" board.

3. **Set of Mixing Bowls**

   Pick a set with at least four glass or stainless steel bowls.

4. **Non-stick Skillet and Oil Spray**

   The dynamic duo for reducing added fat, when cooking, are a non-stick skillet and a refillable oil sprayer. Skillets should have good conducting ability and disperse heat evenly. Choose a 10" skillet and perhaps a 6" pan as well. The oil dispenser allows you to mist the surface of cooking utensils with a fine spray, rather than adding oil by the spoonful.

5. Pots

The minimum required is two pots; a larger one for soup or pasta, a smaller one for sauces or steamed vegetables. Exact sizes depend on the number of persons to be served.

6. Blender

Blenders are extremely useful for puréeing soups, vegetables, dressings, fruit smoothies and soy shakes.

7. Basket Steamer

An inexpensive gadget that fits into almost any size pot is the stainless steel basket steamer, used to steam vegetables or Veggie Wieners. It gives Veggie Wieners a plumpness and juiciness that other cooking methods don't provide. Electric steamers are also available.

8. Colander or Strainer

Use these to drain liquid from cooked pasta, potatoes and cooked or canned legumes.

9. Hand Held Tools

Here are the essentials: can opener, paring knife, potato peeler, measuring cups and spoons, wooden spoon, food grater, pancake flipper, spring-loaded tongs, and whisk. Better quality tools allow you to perform with ease and speed.

10. Food Processor

A food processor is not crucial to preparing the recipes in this book, however this kitchen workhorse saves time in chopping and expands the range of foods you can prepare.

NUTRITIONAL ANALYSIS

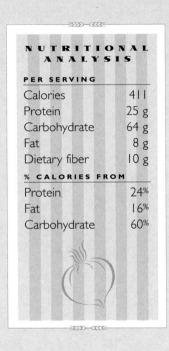

NUTRITIONAL ANALYSIS

PER SERVING

Calories	411
Protein	25 g
Carbohydrate	64 g
Fat	8 g
Dietary fiber	10 g

% CALORIES FROM

Protein	24%
Fat	16%
Carbohydrate	60%

Label readers, nutrition buffs, and weight-conscious individuals who use point systems: here's a section for you!

Our recipes are carefully designed, to provide you with great taste, yet stay within the health guidelines. Yves Veggie Cuisine products are high in protein and essential vitamins and minerals. At the same time, they contain no cholesterol and little or no fat, making it easy for you to 'eat healthy'.

Beside every recipe, you'll find a nutritional analysis. For example, beside the recipe for Shepherd's Pie (page 99) you will see a box like the one shown at the left.

The analysis does not include optional ingredients and where there is a range in amount for an ingredient, the lower amount is used for analysis.

Below the grams of protein, carbohydrate, fat and fiber in each serving, we show the percentage of calories that come from protein, fat and carbohydrate. You have probably heard that not more than 30 percent of your calories should come from fat. This means that the occasional recipe – a salad dressing or favorite entrée – can be above the 30 percent guideline. On average, try to stay within the 30 percent limit. You'll see that our recipes are designed with your health in mind.

Here are The World Health Organization's guidelines for the percent calories from protein, fat, carbohydrate in our overall diet.* This pattern is recommended for adults, to maintain good health and prevent chronic disease. National and international health organizations promote similar guidelines, to help us reduce risk of heart disease, cancer and other chronic diseases.

	LOWER LIMIT % TOTAL CALORIES	UPPER LIMIT % TOTAL CALORIES
Protein	10%	15%
Carbohydrate	55%	75%
Total Fat	15%	30%

Many plant foods – grains, vegetables and fruits – provide 10 percent or less of their calories from fat. They contain healthful plant oils, and little or no saturated fat. Building your diet around these foods helps you keep a healthy balance. Yves products can help too – they are virtually fat free, and free of saturated fat. Since Yves products are excellent sources of protein, our recipes are high in protein too. Add fresh-baked rolls or salad to an item like Shepherd's Pie and there's still room for salad dressing or dessert.

* *Diet, Nutrition and the Prevention of Chronic Diseases, World Health Organization Technical Report Series 797, Geneva*

TWO DIFFERENT CONCEPTS

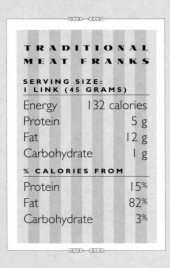

TRADITIONAL MEAT FRANKS

SERVING SIZE:
1 LINK (45 GRAMS)

Energy	132 calories
Protein	5 g
Fat	12 g
Carbohydrate	1 g

% CALORIES FROM

Protein	15%
Fat	82%
Carbohydrate	3%

% FAT (BY WEIGHT) & % CALORIES FROM FAT

Do you find label information confusing? For example, labels list *grams* of protein, fat and carbohydrate per serving. Health experts say you should get 30 percent or less of your *calories* from fat. How do these two concepts fit together? In fact, they are quite different; 30 percent or less of the food's *weight from fat* is not the same as 30 percent or less *calories from fat.* Here's the math, shown below for traditional meat franks and then, for Yves Veggie Wieners.

EXAMPLE #1
TRADITIONAL MEAT FRANKS

% FAT (BY WEIGHT)
Here's how the percentage of fat by weight is calculated:

$$\frac{\text{fat weight (12 grams)}}{\text{total weight (45 grams)}} = \textbf{27\% fat by weight}$$

% CALORIES FROM FAT
Here's how the percentage of calories from fat is calculated*:

5 grams protein x 4 calories per gram	=	20 calories from protein
12 grams fat x 9 calories per gram	=	108 calories from fat
1 gram carbohydrate x 4 calories per gram	=	4 calories from carbohydrate
	Total calories	= 132 calories

$$\text{Percentage of calories from fat is} \quad \frac{108 \text{ calories}}{132 \text{ calories}} = \textbf{82\% calories from fat in this frank}$$

In this traditional frankfurter, 15 percent of the calories come from protein, 3 percent from carbohydrate and 82 percent from fat.

EXAMPLE #2

YVES VEGGIE WIENERS

% FAT (BY WEIGHT)

Here's how the percentage of fat by weight is calculated:

$$\frac{\text{fat weight} \quad (0 \text{ grams})}{\text{total weight (46 grams)}} = \textbf{0\% fat by weight}$$

% CALORIES FROM FAT

Here's how the percentage of calories from fat is calculated*:

11 grams protein × 4 calories per gram	=	44	calories from protein
0 grams fat × 9 calories per gram	=	0	calories from fat
2.2 grams carbohydrate × 4 calories per gram	=	9	calories from carbohydrate
Total calories	=	53	calories

$$\text{Percentage of calories from fat is} \quad \frac{0 \text{ calories}}{53 \text{ calories}} = \textbf{0\% calories from fat in this veggie dog}$$

In the Yves Veggie Wiener, 83 percent of calories come from protein, 17 percent from carbohydrate and 0 percent from fat.

YVES VEGGIE WIENERS	
SERVING SIZE: 1 WIENER (46 GRAMS)	
Energy	53 calories
Protein	11 g
Fat	0 g
Carbohydrate	2.2 g
% CALORIES FROM	
Protein	83%
Fat	0%
Carbohydrate	17%

For calculation: each gram of protein and carbohydrate provides approximately 4 calories, each gram of fat 9 calories. In other words, each gram of fat is loaded with more than twice the calories, when compared with a gram of protein or carbohydrate. Due to rounding rules there may be slight variations in figures.

BREAKFAST

Egg Muffin

Breakfast Burrito

Rancheros Scrambled Egg

Sunny Potato Pancake

Veggie Hash

Veggie Ham and Cheese Omelet

EGG MUFFIN

START YOUR DAY WITH PROTEIN

A report issued by the Food and Agriculture Organization of the United Nations has shed light on how we rate the protein on our plate. This paper, entitled 'Protein Quality Evaluation' was prepared by an international team of scientific experts.* It summarized research on protein-rich foods, and updated our thinking regarding how well different proteins meet our needs. The scientists presented a new scoring method for protein – the PDCAAS or 'Protein Digestibility Corrected Amino Acid Score'. Just try saying that quickly!

Egg has long been considered the nutrition standard, in terms of protein quality. The PDCAAS established that soy protein stands with the best, in terms of protein quality.

The breakfast recipes in this section provide plenty of protein to help you and your family members have high-energy, productive mornings.

*Protein Quality Evaluation, Report of the joint Food and Agriculture Organization of the United States and the World Health Organization, F.A.O. Nutrition paper 51, Rome. 1991.

BREAKFAST: WHO SAYS YOU CAN'T TAKE IT WITH YOU?

No time to sit down for breakfast? The Burrito recipe on page 26 combines the good nutrition of a hearty breakfast with the convenience of a roll-up. Here's what scientific research has shown about the value of starting your day with a substantial breakfast. Those who skip this important meal work less efficiently, display decreased work output and show reduced problem solving ability by late morning. Teachers report that children who have eaten breakfast have better attitudes, longer attention spans and attain higher academic achievement. So prepare it, grab it and go! You'll have a better morning all round.

EGG MUFFIN

This high protein breakfast will get your day off to a good start! And here's a chef's tip to make it even easier. When poaching an egg, add a little salt and vinegar to the cooking water. This helps coagulate the egg and keeps it from dispersing in the water.

2 slices	Yves Canadian Veggie Bacon	1	English muffin
1 quart	water	1 slice	low fat or regular cheddar
2 tbsp	white vinegar		or soy cheese
1 tsp	salt	1 slice	tomato (optional)
1	egg		

For each serving:

1. In small saucepan, bring water, vinegar and salt to a boil; reduce heat so that water is barely simmering.
2. Crack egg into small bowl and carefully slide egg into water.
3. Cook egg to your preference of hardness and remove with slotted spoon.
4. In skillet, sauté Yves Veggie Bacon in oil over medium heat for 1 minute on each side.
5. Meanwhile, toast muffin.
6. On bottom half of muffin, place Yves Veggie Bacon, then egg, cheese, tomato slice (if using) and top half of muffin.

MAKES 1 SERVING

VARIATION: To cut the fat even further, replace the whole egg in this recipe with 2 egg whites, scrambled in a non-stick pan with a little oil spray. Use soy cheese, and your Egg Muffin will be cholesterol-free.

(See photo page 23)

NUTRITIONAL ANALYSIS

PER SERVING

Calories	302
Protein	27 g
Carbohydrate	29 g
Fat	7 g
Dietary fiber	2 g

% CALORIES FROM

Protein	38%
Fat	23%
Carbohydrate	39%

BREAKFAST BURRITO
WITH YVES CANADIAN VEGGIE BACON

Here's a great way to start a weekend. In fact, burritos can be served for breakfast, lunch, dinner, or between meals as a snack. Simply wrap a flour tortilla around a variety of savory ingredients and enjoy! At breakfast, have a glass of orange juice with your burrito. It increases iron absorption from this nourishing dish.

2 slices	Yves Canadian Veggie Bacon	¼ cup	salsa
½–1 tsp	olive oil (or spray)	¼ cup	chopped green onion
2	medium eggs or	¼ cup	shredded cheddar cheese
	2 egg whites		(optional)
Pinch	salt	2	10" soft whole wheat
Pinch	pepper		tortilla shells

1. In large non-stick skillet, sauté Yves Canadian Veggie Bacon in oil over medium heat for 1 minute on each side. Place Yves Veggie Bacon on cutting board and slice into diagonal (julienne) slices.
2. Crack eggs in bowl, add salt and pepper and whisk with fork for one minute.
3. Place skillet over medium heat, pour in eggs and cook, stirring frequently, until eggs are scrambled. Remove eggs from skillet, reduce heat to low and return pan to heat.
4. Place one tortilla in skillet. Spoon half the scrambled egg in strip from left to right on tortilla. Spread half the salsa over eggs. Sprinkle half the green onions, cheese (if using) and Yves Veggie Bacon along strip of eggs.
5. Slide tortilla onto cutting board. To prevent filling from falling out while eating, fold 2" of right side of tortilla shell towards center. Snugly roll tortilla over top of filling and away from you, to form a roll. Repeat for second tortilla.

MAKES 2 BURRITOS

VARIATION: Fill each burrito with one half cup of cooked rice and one half cup of Veggie Mexi Mix (page 105).

NUTRITIONAL ANALYSIS

PER BURRITO

Calories	352
Protein	18 g
Carbohydrate	44 g
Fat	11 g
Dietary fiber	4 g

% CALORIES FROM

Protein	21%
Fat	29%
Carbohydrate	50%

PER BURRITO WITH EGG WHITE

Calories	299
Protein	16 g
Carbohydrate	44 g
Fat	6 g
Dietary fiber	4 g

% CALORIES FROM

Protein	22%
Fat	19%
Carbohydrate	59%

RANCHEROS SCRAMBLED EGGS

WITH YVES VEGGIE BREAKFAST LINKS

The name of this recipe is taken from Huevos Rancheros, meaning "Rancher's Eggs" in Spanish. The original recipe consisted of fried corn tortillas, topped with fried eggs, followed by a layer of salsa. This juicy, lighter version can be made with egg whites or whole eggs; either way it's an excellent source of protein to start your day.

1	Yves Veggie Breakfast Link, or Yves Canadian Veggie Bacon slice, diced	1–2 tsp	olive oil
		2 tbsp	diced fresh tomato
		1 tbsp	chopped green onion
2	egg whites or eggs	2 tsp	cilantro
1 tbsp	yogurt	1/4 tsp	ground cumin
Pinch	salt	Pinch	oregano leaves
Pinch	pepper	2 slices	whole wheat toast

1. Beat egg whites or eggs, yogurt, salt and pepper with fork in medium bowl for 1 minute.
2. In skillet, sauté Yves Breakfast Links or Yves Veggie Bacon in oil over medium heat for 1 minute.
3. Add tomato, green onion and sauté for 30 seconds.
4. Stir in cilantro, cumin and oregano.
5. Add egg mixture and stir quickly until scrambled. Serve with whole wheat toast.

MAKES 1 SERVING

NUTRITIONAL ANALYSIS

PER SERVING WITH EGG WHITE

Calories	295
Protein	26 g
Carbohydrate	33 g
Fat	7 g
Dietary fiber	5 g

% CALORIES FROM

Protein	34%
Fat	22%
Carbohydrate	44%

PER SERVING WITH EGG

Calories	400
Protein	30 g
Carbohydrate	34 g
Fat	17 g
Dietary fiber	5 g

% CALORIES FROM

Protein	30%
Fat	37%
Carbohydrate	33%

SUNNY POTATO PANCAKES

SUNNY POTATO PANCAKE

WITH YVES VEGGIE HAM

Potatoes and red peppers are high in vitamin C, and Yves products contribute protein, making this pancake very nutritious – not to mention tasty! This recipe is a little more complex than some, but the end result is well worth the effort. It can be served at breakfast, brunch or as a side dish for dinner.

4 slices	Yves Veggie Ham or Yves Canadian Veggie Bacon	1/2	red bell pepper, sliced into thin strips
2	large Russet or Idaho potatoes, peeled and grated	1/4 tsp	salt
1/4 tsp	salt	Pinch	fresh ground black pepper
1/2	medium onion, sliced into thin strips	1/4 tsp	thyme leaves
		1 tbsp	olive oil
1/4 cup	green onions, chopped	1/4 cup	low-fat sour cream (optional)

1. Cut Yves Veggie Ham or Yves Veggie Bacon in half. Place both halves on top of each other and cut into thin strips. Set aside.
2. Combine potato and salt together in medium bowl and mix well. Set aside for 10 minutes.
3. Meanwhile, in small (6") non-stick skillet, sauté onion, red peppers, green onions, salt, pepper, thyme and Yves Veggie Ham or Yves Veggie Bacon in 1/2 tbsp olive oil for 5 minutes or until tender. Set vegetable mixture aside.
4. Remove excess moisture from potatoes by tightly squeezing small handfuls of potatoes. (This step is important.)
5. Add remaining oil to skillet and press half of potatoes in skillet followed by vegetable mixture and top with remaining potatoes. Press down to form a round pancake.
6. Cook over medium heat for 5 minutes or until golden brown. Do not stir. Place plate over top of skillet. Turn skillet upside down to catch pancake on plate. Slide back into skillet to cook reverse side for 5 minutes or until golden brown.
7. Serve warm with sour cream (if using).

MAKES 2 SERVINGS

NUTRITIONAL ANALYSIS

PER SERVING

Calories	263
Protein	12 g
Carbohydrate	40 g
Fat	9 g
Dietary fiber	5 g

% CALORIES FROM

Protein	18%
Fat	24%
Carbohydrate	58%

VEGGIE HASH
W I T H   Y V E S   V E G G I E   G R O U N D   R O U N D

Traditionally, hash was a way of serving up leftovers. The recipe below is so tasty that you won't have leftovers from this meal. The key to developing and deepening the overall flavor is to slowly sauté onion and cabbage until they are browned and the potatoes are crusty, before adding Yves Veggie Ground Round.

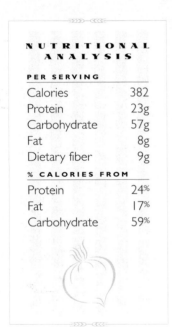

1 pkg	Yves Veggie Ground Round	6 cups	cooked, diced Idaho
2 tbsp	bread crumbs		potatoes (about 4
1/2	medium onion, diced		medium potatoes)
2 tbsp	olive oil	1/4 tsp	salt
1 cup	diced cabbage	Pinch	pepper

1. In medium bowl, crumble Yves Veggie Ground Round with fork, add bread crumbs and mix well. Set aside.
2. In skillet over medium heat, sauté onion in oil for 5 minutes or until onion starts to brown. Add cabbage and potatoes; continue cooking until potatoes are heated through and begin to become crusty.
3. Stir in salt, pepper and Yves Veggie Ground Round mixture. Cook 5 minutes, stirring occasionally. Season to taste.

MAKES 4 SERVINGS

VARIATION: For added color, add 1/4 cup diced red pepper along with the cabbage and potato.

VEGGIE HAM & CHEESE OMELET
MADE WITH YVES VEGGIE HAM

Omelets are a versatile dish for breakfast, lunch or brunch. They can incorporate all sorts of savory ingredients such as Yves Veggie Ham or Yves Veggie Breakfast Links. For best results, use a non-stick pan, well-seasoned skillet or omelet pan. For a variety of great tasting omelets try different combinations of vegetables, for example asparagus, tomatoes or mushrooms and fresh herbs such as basil, dill or tarragon. Omelets tend to be a little high in fat; health conscious people can achieve balance over the course of a day with grains, vegetables, fruit, and low fat items such as Yves products.

2 slices	Yves Veggie Ham or Yves Veggie Breakfast Links, diced	1 tsp	olive oil
		2 tbsp	grated cheddar cheese
2	eggs	1 tbsp	finely chopped green onion
Pinch	salt	2 slices	whole wheat toast
Pinch	pepper		

1. Crack eggs in large bowl, add salt and pepper and whisk with fork until frothy. Set aside.
2. Heat oil in skillet over medium high heat. Add eggs and stir constantly for approximately 15 seconds or until the omelet is set.
3. Sprinkle Yves Veggie Ham, cheese and green onion in strip along center of omelet. Cook for 30 seconds. Be careful not to overcook bottom of omelet. With spatula, fold omelet in half and slide onto serving plate. Cut toast in half diagonally and serve with omelet.

MAKES 1 SERVING

NUTRITIONAL ANALYSIS

PER SERVING

Calories	417
Protein	27 g
Carbohydrate	31 g
Fat	21 g
Dietary fiber	4g

% CALORIES FROM

Protein	26%
Fat	46%
Carbohydrate	28%

APPETIZERS & SNACKS

Veggie Bacon Tortilla Oriana

Swedish Veggie Meatballs

Yves Hawaiian Pizza Squares

Veggie Ground Round Nachos

Antipasto Salad Platter

Gyozas (Potstickers)

Gyoza Dipping Sauce

VEGGIE BACON TORTILLA ORIANA

SNACKING CAN BE GOOD FOR YOU!

Here are snacks and appetizers that are quick to put together – and healthy too! They can boost your energy level between meals and give you staying power. For children with small appetites, athletes and busy adults, snacks can be as important as meals in providing protein, energy, vitamins and minerals to the diet. Make sure your snacks count!

YVES PIZZA IS A HEALTHY FOOD, FOR KIDS AND ADULTS ALIKE

Can a food do all these things:
- ❑ be a favorite with children and adults,
- ❑ be assembled in 8 minutes – even by children,
- ❑ include all food groups?

Yes! Follow the recipe on page 37 (for speed, use a ready made crust) and your pizza will include good nutrition from every food group.

BREAD, CEREAL, RICE, AND PASTA FOODS

Breads and similar foods made from grains are high in complex carbohydrate, which is the body's favorite fuel. It is recommended that children consume at least half their daily calories from grain products – and this can definitely include pizza crust!

VEGETABLES AND FRUIT

These colorful foods are packed with the vitamins and minerals needed to protect immune systems, build strong bodies, regulate heartbeat, and pass messages along nerve cells. Green pepper contains important antioxidants such as the vitamins A and C. Pineapple provides more vitamin C; mushrooms add some trace minerals.

MILK AND MILK PRODUCTS

The calcium found in cheddar cheese and mozzarella helps to build strong bones and teeth and to support muscle and nerve function.

MEAT ALTERNATIVES, BEANS AND NUTS

All of these provide protein that is used to repair and maintain body tissues, produce hemoglobin, and build antibodies, enzymes, and hormones. Yves Canadian Veggie Bacon is high in protein (16 grams in 3 slices), and it's fortified with Vitamin B12, too.

Remember – favorite snacks can be simple and packed with good nutrition!

VEGGIE BACON TORTILLA ORIANA
WITH YVES CANADIAN VEGGIE BACON

This recipe is so simple, yet it is a wonderful combination of tastes and textures. It is best prepared ahead of time, and allowed to sit before serving, making it easier to slice. If you like, serve it with any or all of the following sauces: salsa, sour cream and guacamole.

8 slices	Yves Canadian Veggie Bacon	4	10" soft flour tortillas
½ cup	Cajun or spicy tomato sauce	½ cup	grated low fat or regular mozzarella or soy cheese

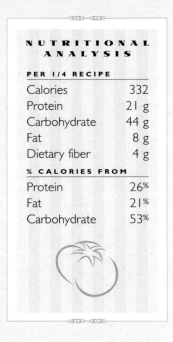

NUTRITIONAL ANALYSIS

PER 1/4 RECIPE

Calories	332
Protein	21 g
Carbohydrate	44 g
Fat	8 g
Dietary fiber	4 g

% CALORIES FROM

Protein	26%
Fat	21%
Carbohydrate	53%

1. Brush or spread about 2 tbsp of tomato sauce on each tortilla.
2. Starting at one end of tortilla, place 2 slices Yves Veggie Bacon next to each other, lengthwise.
3. Top with 2 tbsp cheese.
4. Start at same end of tortilla and roll tightly.
5. Refrigerate until ready to serve. If preparing a day ahead, wrap in plastic.
6. Place a piece of foil on a cookie sheet. Remove plastic wrap from tortillas and bake in 350°F oven until cheese is melted, about 12 minutes. Remove from oven and cut into 1" rounds.
7. If desired, serve with salsa, sour cream or guacamole.

MAKES 3–4 SERVINGS

(See photo page 33)

SWEDISH VEGGIE MEATBALLS
WITH YVES VEGGIE GROUND ROUND

These veggie meatballs in a creamy gravy may be used as an appetizer or they will serve three people as an entrée, over rice or with noodles. Swedish meatballs have a distinctive flavor due to the use of dill.

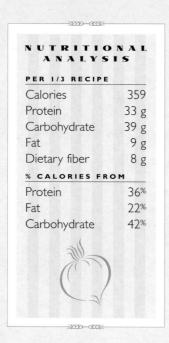

NUTRITIONAL ANALYSIS

PER 1/3 RECIPE

Calories	359
Protein	33 g
Carbohydrate	39 g
Fat	9 g
Dietary fiber	8 g

% CALORIES FROM

Protein	36%
Fat	22%
Carbohydrate	42%

1	recipe for Veggie Meatballs, (see recipe page 91)	1 tsp	dill weed
1/2	medium onion, diced	1/4 tsp	oregano
1–2 tbsp	olive oil	1/4 tsp	nutmeg
1/2 cup	stock or white wine	1/8 tsp	pepper
1/4 cup	all-purpose flour	3 tbsp	ketchup
3 cups	vegetable stock	1 1/2 tbsp	Dijon mustard
		1/4 cup	low-fat sour cream

1. Make Veggie Meatballs (recipe page 91).
2. While meatballs are baking, sauté onion in oil in skillet, over medium heat, for 5 minutes or until soft.
3. Add 1/2 cup stock or wine and cook about 4 minutes to reduce liquid to half volume. Mix in flour and stir constantly for 3 minutes to prevent flour from burning.
4. Remove from heat for 2 minutes and slowly stir in 1/2 cup of stock. Return to heat and gradually add more stock as flour absorbs liquid.
5. Add dill weed, oregano, nutmeg, pepper, ketchup, and mustard.
6. Bring to boil, reduce heat and simmer for 10 minutes.
7. Place cream in small bowl along with 1 cup of thickened broth. (See blurb on page 98). Mix and return to pan along with meatballs. Heat through but do not boil.

MAKES 12–18 MEATBALLS

VARIATION: Serve over rice or flat noodles, such as fettuccini or broad egg noodles, for a main course.

YVES HAWAIIAN PIZZA SQUARES

WITH YVES CANADIAN VEGGIE BACON

For this thick-crusted pizza appetizer, dough made from the recipe on page 102 is a very flavorful choice. Ready-made pizza shells from your local supermarket, are a convenient alternative. Assembling pizzas together is a pleasant activity with family and guests of all ages.

1 pkg	Yves Canadian Veggie Bacon, or Yves Veggie Ham 1/2" dice	1 cup	pineapple pieces, squeezed to remove excess liquid
1 tsp	olive oil or spray	1/2 cup	grated low-fat mozzarella cheese
1 recipe	Pizza Dough, (see recipe page 102) or 2 pre-made 12" pizza shells	1/4 cup	grated parmesan cheese
		2 tsp	olive oil (optional)
1 1/2 cup	your favorite pizza sauce		

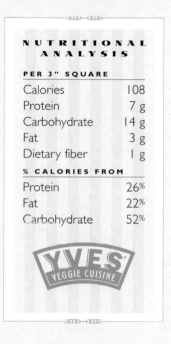

NUTRITIONAL ANALYSIS

PER 3" SQUARE

Calories	108
Protein	7 g
Carbohydrate	14 g
Fat	3 g
Dietary fiber	1 g

% CALORIES FROM

Protein	26%
Fat	22%
Carbohydrate	52%

YVES
VEGGIE CUISINE

1. Preheat oven to 425°F.
2. Use 1 tsp oil or spray to lightly oil baking tray (approximately 10 x 15" tray).
3. Press out pizza dough evenly to all corners of tray.
4. Spread pizza sauce across dough.
5. Evenly sprinkle pineapple pieces, followed by Yves Veggie Bacon, mozzarella and parmesan cheese.
6. Drizzle remaining 2 tsp olive oil (if using) along edge of pizza dough.
7. Bake for 16 minutes or until crust is golden brown. (If using ready-made shell, follow package directions for baking.)
8. Cut into 3" squares.

MAKES 15 SQUARES

VARIATION: In place of Yves Canadian Veggie Bacon, use 1 to 1 1/2 packages of Yves Veggie Pizza Pepperoni.

VEGGIE GROUND ROUND NACHOS
WITH YVES VEGGIE GROUND ROUND

Do you think of nachos as a nutritious snack? They are when you use this recipe! You'll get plenty of iron, zinc and protein from Yves Veggie Ground Round. Cheese provides calcium. Baked tortilla chips count as a serving of grain, and you even get some veggies with the tomato salsa, onions and olives. So munch away!

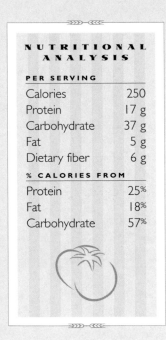

NUTRITIONAL ANALYSIS

PER SERVING

Calories	250
Protein	17 g
Carbohydrate	37 g
Fat	5 g
Dietary fiber	6 g

% CALORIES FROM

Protein	25%
Fat	18%
Carbohydrate	57%

¹/₂ pkg	Yves Veggie Ground Round	¹/₄ cup	sliced black olives
¹/₄ cup	salsa	¹/₄ cup	chopped green onions
¹/₈ tsp	ground cumin		
4 cups	baked or regular	**GARNISH ON SIDE** (optional)	
(5 oz)	tortilla chips	¹/₂ cup	salsa
¹/₂ cup	grated low-fat mozzarella cheese	¹/₂ cup	sour cream

1. Preheat oven to 400°F.
2. Mash Yves Veggie Ground Round in medium bowl with fork and stir in salsa and cumin. Set aside.
3. Arrange half of the nacho chips on an ovenproof platter.
4. Sprinkle half of each of the following ingredients over nacho chips: Yves Veggie Ground Round mixture, cheese, olives and green onions.
5. Arrange remaining chips, Yves Veggie Ground Round mixture, olives and green onions.
6. Sprinkle top with remaining cheese.
7. Bake for 10–15 minutes or until cheese is melted and chips just start to brown.
8. Serve hot with salsa and sour cream (if using) on the side.

MAKES 4 SERVINGS

ANTIPASTO SALAD PLATTER
WITH YVES VEGGIE PEPPERONI

In Italian, antipasto means 'before the meal'. A more lighthearted and romantic description likens these nibbles to the little kisses that precede a great love affair. Antipasto may be topped with a little of your favorite low fat dressing or Balsamic Vinaigrette (page 55). This dish can be served as an appetizer, a delicious snack or party food, or the main meal at lunch, accompanied by savory flat bread and perhaps a bowl of soup.

4 slices	Yves Veggie Pepperoni or Yves Veggie Deli Slices	3	whole green olives
3	leafy lettuce leaves	3	whole black olives
1 cup	green beans, blanched	1/2 cup	feta cheese (optional)
6	tomato wedges	2–3 tbsp	low-fat dressing or
3	artichoke hearts, halved		Balsamic Vinaigrette (see recipe page 55)

1. Cut Yves Veggie Pepperoni or Yves Deli Slices into 1/4" strips and set aside.
2. On platter or plate, form bed of lettuce. Artistically arrange beans, tomatoes, artichoke hearts and olives. Sprinkle cheese (if using) followed by Yves Deli Slices.
3. Sprinkle dressing over salad.

MAKES 2 SERVINGS

VARIATION: Add any of the following ingredients in appropriate amounts:
❑ Roasted or grilled eggplant, zucchini, red and yellow bell peppers
❑ Marinated sun dried tomatoes, mushrooms or other favorite vegetables.

NUTRITIONAL ANALYSIS

PER SERVING (WITHOUT DRESSING AND CHEESE)

Calories	125
Protein	12 g
Carbohydrate	16 g
Fat	2 g
Dietary fiber	4 g

% CALORIES FROM

Protein	35%
Fat	16%
Carbohydrate	49%

PER SERVING (WITH CHEESE)

Calories	225
Protein	17 g
Carbohydrate	17 g
Fat	10 g
Dietary fiber	4 g

% CALORIES FROM

Protein	29%
Fat	40%
Carbohydrate	31%

GYOZAS (POTSTICKERS)
WITH YVES GARDEN VEGETABLE PATTIES

Making Gyozas (also known as Potstickers) is like wrapping little gifts, so this recipe is fun to do with children. They (and you) will also enjoy dipping Gyozas into one or more sauces. Although this recipe suggests a teriyaki-based dipping sauce, you may also use your favorite plum, barbecue or peanut sauce. Wonton wrappers are small circles or squares made from flour. Packages of wonton wrappers are sold in produce sections of large food stores and in Oriental markets. Gyozas freeze well, so make a big batch. When hunger strikes or guests arrive, you can quickly heat them in a pan, for instant, healthy snacks.

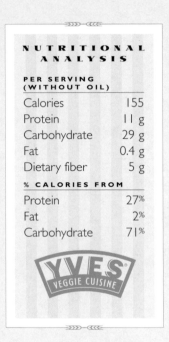

NUTRITIONAL ANALYSIS

PER SERVING (WITHOUT OIL)

Calories	155
Protein	11 g
Carbohydrate	29 g
Fat	0.4 g
Dietary fiber	5 g

% CALORIES FROM

Protein	27%
Fat	2%
Carbohydrate	71%

4	Yves Garden Vegetable Patties	1 pkg	wonton wrappers (65)
¼ cup	chopped green onions	¼ cup	water
1 tbsp	minced ginger		olive oil (spray or small amount)
1 tbsp	chopped cilantro		Gyoza Dipping Sauce
3 tbsp	teriyaki sauce		(see recipe on next page)
	salt and pepper to taste		

1. In medium bowl, mash Yves Garden Vegetable Patties with fork. Add green onion, ginger, cilantro, teriyaki sauce, salt, pepper and mix well.
2. Separate wonton wrappers and lay them on counter. Brush a little water along the edge of each wrapper.
3. Place one spoonful of Vegetable Patty mixture in the middle of each wrapper. Fold in half diagonally to form a triangle or semi circle. Press firmly along edges to close the Gyozas.
4. Lightly oil non-stick pan and brown Gyozas for 2 minutes on each side. Add ¼ cup of water and cover. Simmer on medium heat for 2 or 3 minutes or until water has evaporated. Serve with Gyoza Dipping Sauce or other sauces.

MAKES 4 SERVINGS

Stores often stock two types of teriyaki sauce: thick teriyaki glaze that is used for barbecues, and thin teriyaki sauce, with the consistency of soy sauce, that is required for this recipe. As a variation, you may add minced ginger or cilantro to deepen the flavor.

1 cup	teriyaki sauce	2 tbsp	brown sugar
1 tbsp	toasted sesame oil	½ cup	water

1. In saucepan, mix teriyaki sauce, oil and sugar; bring to a boil, reduce heat and simmer for 5 minutes.
2. Remove from heat and add water. Let cool for 2 minutes. Serve with Gyozas. This sauce will keep, refrigerated, for up to three weeks.

MAKES 1 CUP

PARTY WITHOUT PUTTING ON THE POUNDS

Is this possible? Yes, and here are six tips to help you succeed.

1. Exercise before the party – your higher metabolic rate will burn more calories.
2. When your blood sugar is low, how much self-control do you have? None. So eat low-fat, high-nutrition meals earlier in the day.
3. For potluck events, bring something tasty and low-fat such as Yves Deli Slices or Yves Pepperoni, crusty rye bread and a jar of Dijon mustard. This is light eating at its best!
4. Don't stand beside the nut bowl or the tray of sausage rolls. Take a small plateful of foods such as raw veggies and Yves Gyozas and head for the other side of the room.
5. Drink sparkling water or club soda and use them to dilute high calorie beverages.
6. Explore what there is to enjoy apart from food: music, dancing and good company.

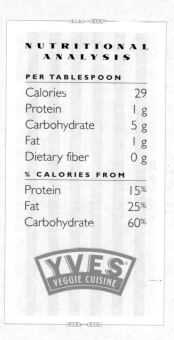

NUTRITIONAL ANALYSIS

PER TABLESPOON

Calories	29
Protein	1 g
Carbohydrate	5 g
Fat	1 g
Dietary fiber	0 g

% CALORIES FROM

Protein	15%
Fat	25%
Carbohydrate	60%

YVES
VEGGIE CUISINE

SOUPS & SALADS

Borscht with Fresh Dill

Split Pea Soup

Smoky Potato and Broccoli Soup

Minestrone Soup

Hearty Alsacienne Lentil Soup

Paprika Vegetable Soup

Pasta Salad Primavera

Caesar Salad

Caesar Dressing

Chef Salad

Balsamic Vinaigrette

Spinach Salad with Veggie Bacon Bits

Creamy Basil Dressing

Creamy Dill Mayo

Tomato-Basil Dressing

Veggie Bacon Bits

BORSCHT WITH FRESH DILL

HEROES OF THE NUTRITION WORLD –
THE ANTIOXIDANTS: VITAMINS A, C & E

It may come as a surprise that one of the biggest threats to your body is the same substance that you depend on for life – oxygen! During normal body processes, some oxygen molecules lose an electron and become unstable, turning into potentially harmful free radicals. Free radicals are thought to cause many diseases from cancers to colds, for example by damaging a person's DNA and causing unwanted changes in the basic building blocks of cells. This damage can often be prevented and sometimes reversed by the healing properties of antioxidants. Antioxidants are the focus of much scientific interest, due to their ability to stabilize free radicals in the body by giving an electron.

Beta-carotene, a close relative of vitamin A, acts as a free radical scavenger to protect cells. It can prevent oxidation of LDL ('bad') cholesterol, a significant stage on the slippery slope to heart disease. Beta-carotene is most commonly found in the bright yellow, orange and green vegetables and fruits, for example leafy greens, carrots, sweet potatoes, squash and papaya. Other colorful veggies contain related antioxidants.

Ascorbic acid, found in vegetables and citrus fruits, is more commonly called vitamin C. It acts as an antioxidant by scavenging and quenching free radicals throughout the body.

Vitamin E is present in vegetables, nuts, seeds, oils, soybeans and whole grains. Its antioxidant function is important in protecting red blood cells. Vitamin E may also be important in reducing sunburn severity, as well as the lines and wrinkles associated with sun exposure.

Next time you walk down the produce aisle, feast your eyes on the colorful, antioxidant-rich fruits and veggies. Then fill your basket, and include some nuts and soyfoods. When free radicals set out to create havoc, you'll be prepared!

BORSCHT WITH FRESH DILL
WITH YVES CANADIAN VEGGIE BACON

Native to Russia and Poland, beet-based Borscht brings a burst of color to any dinner table. This soup has a delicate smoky flavor from Yves Canadian Veggie Bacon, mingled with dill and a pleasant combination of vegetables. (You can get your 5-a-day right here!) Serve this soup hot in winter, with dark rye bread, or cold in summer, accompanied by a crispy salad.

2 slices	Yves Canadian Veggie Bacon	1 cup	diced potato
1–2 tbsp	olive oil	1	bay leaf
1	medium onion, diced	2 tbsp	chopped parsley
1/2 cup	diced carrots	2 tbsp	chopped fresh dill weed
1/2 cup	diced celery	2 tsp	red wine vinegar
2 tbsp	tomato paste	1/8 tsp	black pepper
4 cups	vegetable stock	1 cup	sour cream (optional)
2 cups	diced beets	4	lemon wedges (optional)
1 cup	shredded green cabbage		

1. In saucepan, sauté Yves Veggie Bacon in oil for 1 minute on each side, remove, slice into 1/2" dice and set aside.
2. Add onions, carrots, celery and sauté for 3 minutes.
3. Add tomato paste, cook for 1 minute then add diced Yves Veggie Bacon, stock, beets, cabbage, potatoes, bay leaf, bring to simmer and cook for 10 minutes or until potatoes are cooked.
4. Mix together parsley, dill, vinegar, pepper and sour cream (if using).
5. Stir one cup of hot liquid into the herb mix and add to soup.
6. Adjust seasoning, bring to simmer (do not boil) and serve with fresh dill sprig and lemon wedges (if using).

MAKES 4 – 6 SERVINGS

(See photo page 43)

NUTRITIONAL ANALYSIS

PER 1/4 RECIPE

Calories	143
Protein	8 g
Carbohydrate	21 g
Fat	5 g
Dietary fiber	4 g

% CALORIES FROM

Protein	20%
Fat	27%
Carbohydrate	53%

PER SERVING WITH CREAM

Calories	263
Protein	10 g
Carbohydrate	25 g
Fat	17 g
Dietary fiber	4 g

% CALORIES FROM

Protein	13%
Fat	52%
Carbohydrate	35%

SPLIT PEA SOUP

WITH YVES CANADIAN VEGGIE BACON

Peas were a dietary staple in Britain as early as the 11th century, and thick pea soup was referred to in the ancient rhyme that begins "Pease porridge hot, pease porridge cold...." Though Britons evidently ate pea soup at different temperatures, we prefer them in this warming and bountiful soup that provides plenty of protein, vitamin A, thiamin, niacin, folate, iron, magnesium, phosphorus, zinc and fiber.

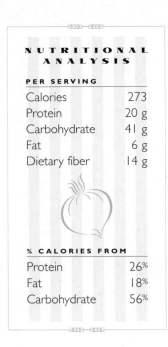

NUTRITIONAL ANALYSIS

PER SERVING

Calories	273
Protein	20 g
Carbohydrate	41 g
Fat	6 g
Dietary fiber	14 g

% CALORIES FROM

Protein	26%
Fat	18%
Carbohydrate	56%

2 slices	Yves Canadian Veggie Bacon, ¼" dice	I cup	dried green split peas, rinsed
½ cup	diced carrot	3	bay leaves
½ cup	diced celery	4	whole cloves
½	medium onion, diced	1/2 tsp	salt
2	cloves garlic, minced	1/8 tsp	black pepper
I tbsp	olive oil	I tbsp	chopped fresh parsley
8 cups	vegetable stock		

1. In saucepan, sauté carrot, celery, onion and garlic in oil over medium heat for 5 minutes.
2. Stir in stock, split peas, bay leaves and cloves. Bring to boil, cover, reduce heat and simmer for 50 – 60 minutes or until peas are cooked and completely disintegrated.
3. Add salt, pepper and Yves Veggie Bacon and heat through. If soup is too thick, add more vegetable stock or water.
4. Garnish with parsley, adjust the seasoning and serve.

MAKES 4 SERVINGS

SMOKY POTATO & BROCCOLI SOUP

WITH YVES CANADIAN VEGGIE BACON

There are several good reasons for broccoli's popularity with health enthusiasts. First, it's loaded with phytochemicals – those plant chemicals that protect us from disease. Second, the calcium in broccoli – and in kale, collards, bok choy, Chinese cabbage and okra – is easy for the body to absorb. This simple soup derives calcium from both broccoli and dairy products. Keep the broccoli stalks, as they can be peeled and the tender centers steamed as a side dish.

2 slices	Yves Canadian Veggie Bacon, 1/2" dice	2 cups	potatoes, 1/4" dice
1–2 tbsp	olive oil	2 cups	small broccoli florets
1/2	medium onion, diced	1 cup	milk
1/2 cup	celery, diced	1/2 cup	heavy cream (optional)
3 tbsp	all-purpose flour	1/4 tsp	salt
5 cups	hot vegetable stock	Pinch	pepper
		1 tbsp	chopped parsley

1. In saucepan, sauté Yves Veggie Bacon, onion and celery in oil over medium heat for 5 minutes or until onions are soft.
2. Stir in flour and cook for 2 minutes, stirring constantly. Remove saucepan from heat for two minutes.
3. Add 1/2 cup of stock, stirring until flour absorbs liquid and mixture is smooth. Continue adding liquid until all stock is added to pot.
4. Return saucepan to heat and add potatoes. Bring soup to boil, reduce heat to simmer and cook for 10 minutes or until potatoes are cooled.
5. Add broccoli and cook for 5 minutes.
6. In bowl or small saucepan, combine hot milk, cream (if using), salt, pepper and parsley. Add 1–2 cups of hot soup stock to this milk mixture and return milk blend to pot. This prevents milk from curdling when it is added to the hot soup.
7. Heat through (without boiling), adjust seasoning and serve.

MAKES 4 SERVINGS

NUTRITIONAL ANALYSIS

PER SERVING

Calories	202
Protein	11 g
Carbohydrate	28 g
Fat	7 g
Dietary fiber	3 g

% CALORIES FROM

Protein	20%
Fat	29%
Carbohydrate	51%

PER SERVING WITH CREAM

Calories	263
Protein	11 g
Carbohydrate	28 g
Fat	13 g
Dietary fiber	3 g

% CALORIES FROM

Protein	16%
Fat	43%
Carbohydrate	41%

MINESTRONE SOUP

WITH YVES CANADIAN VEGGIE BACON

Minestrone, meaning 'big soup' in Italian, is a favorite part of the Mediterranean diet. It generally contains beans, pasta and tomatoes. As in most recipes, amounts of ingredients can be considered a guideline, rather than a formula written in stone, so you may vary amounts to suit your preference. This soup is well balanced, with plenty of vitamins, minerals and protein. At the same time it's a very low-fat choice.

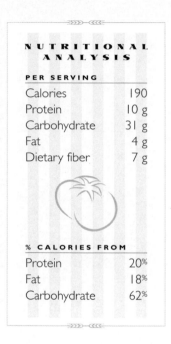

NUTRITIONAL ANALYSIS

PER SERVING

Calories	190
Protein	10 g
Carbohydrate	31 g
Fat	4 g
Dietary fiber	7 g

% CALORIES FROM

Protein	20%
Fat	18%
Carbohydrate	62%

3 slices	Yves Canadian Veggie Bacon or Yves Veggie Pepperoni, 1/2" dice	1 cup	zucchini, diced
		2 cups	chopped fresh or canned tomatoes
1	medium onion, diced	1/4 cup	macaroni noodles
1 cup	diced carrot	2 tbsp	tomato paste
1 cup	diced celery	1 tsp	dried basil
2	cloves garlic, minced	1/2 tsp	salt
1–2 tbsp	olive oil	Pinch	pepper
5 cups	vegetable stock	1/2 cup	cooked white beans
1 cup	green cabbage, chopped	2 tbsp	chopped parsley
1 cup	potato, diced		

1. In large saucepan, sauté onion, carrots, celery and garlic in oil over medium heat for 5 minutes.
2. Stir in stock, cabbage, potato, zucchini, tomatoes, macaroni, tomato paste, basil, salt and pepper.
3. Cover, reduce heat and simmer for about 15–20 minutes or until potato and macaroni are cooked.
4. Add white beans, Yves Veggie Bacon and heat through.
5. Adjust seasoning and garnish with parsley.

MAKES 4 SERVINGS

HEARTY ALSACIENNE LENTIL SOUP

WITH YVES CANADIAN VEGGIE BACON

Since people began farming over 10,000 years ago, lentils have been a favorite crop. This soup, made with small French lentils or larger green lentils, is high in protein, B vitamins, iron, zinc, magnesium, and one serving provides more than half your recommended intake of fiber for the day. This flavorful, nourishing soup is also extremely low in fat.

3 slices	Yves Canadian Veggie Bacon, 1/4" dice	1	celery stick, diced
2	Yves Tofu Wieners or Yves Veggie Wieners, cut in 1/4" cubes	1	medium potato, peeled & diced
		1/3 cup	French lentils or green lentils
2	garlic cloves, finely chopped	3 cups	vegetable broth
1	small onion, diced	1	bay leaf
1 1/2 tbsp	olive oil		salt
1 1/2	carrot, diced		pepper
1	small turnip, peeled & diced		

1. In saucepan, sauté Yves Veggie Bacon, garlic, and onion in olive oil over medium heat for 2 minutes.
2. Add carrots, turnip, celery, and sauté over medium to low heat for another 3 minutes.
3. Add potato, lentils, broth and bay leaf, cover and bring to boil. Reduce heat and simmer for 45 minutes or until lentils are tender.
4. Add Yves Wieners and simmer 1 minute.
5. Season to taste with salt and pepper.

MAKES 4 SERVINGS

NUTRITIONAL ANALYSIS

PER SERVING

Calories	205
Protein	15 g
Carbohydrate	26 g
Fat	6 g
Dietary fiber	5 g

% CALORIES FROM

Protein	28%
Fat	25%
Carbohydrate	47%

PAPRIKA VEGETABLE SOUP
WITH YVES VEGGIE DELI SLICES

This delicious soup was developed using Hungarian paprika, widely considered to be the most aromatic and flavorful. Paprika and caraway give authentic Hungarian flavor, making this another great way to eat your veggies for the day!

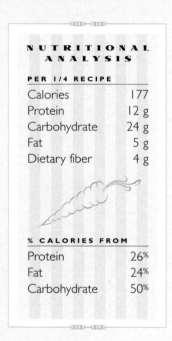

NUTRITIONAL ANALYSIS

PER 1/4 RECIPE

Calories	177
Protein	12 g
Carbohydrate	24 g
Fat	5 g
Dietary fiber	4 g

% CALORIES FROM

Protein	26%
Fat	24%
Carbohydrate	50%

5 slices	Yves Veggie Deli Slices, 1/4" dice	1 1/2 cups	diced potatoes
3 slices	Yves Veggie Pepperoni, 1/4" dice	1 cup	canned tomatoes, drained & chopped
1–2 tbsp	olive oil	2 tsp	paprika
1/2	medium onion, diced	1 tsp	caraway seeds
1 cup	diced carrot	1/2 tsp	salt
1/2 cup	diced celery	1/4 tsp	marjoram
1/2 cup	diced parsnips or celeriac	1/4 tsp	pepper
4 cups	vegetable stock	Pinch	chili pepper flakes (optional)
		1 tbsp	chopped parsley

1. In saucepan, sauté onion, carrot, celery, and parsnips in oil over medium heat for 5 minutes.
2. Add stock, potatoes, tomatoes, paprika, caraway seeds, salt, marjoram, pepper and chili pepper flakes (if using).
3. Bring to boil, reduce heat and simmer for 15 minutes.
4. Add Yves Deli Slices and Yves Veggie Pepperoni and cook for 10 minutes or until potatoes are tender.
5. Add parsley and adjust the seasoning.

MAKES 4–6 SERVINGS

PASTA SALAD PRIMAVERA

WITH YVES VEGGIE PEPPERONI

For this large, colorful salad, we have suggested the use of raw
carrots, cauliflower, broccoli and bell peppers. Alternatively, all
or some of these vegetables may be blanched briefly, making
them softer to the bite and brightening their colors. (See page 13
for definition of blanching.) Note that the dressing for this salad
is entirely without oil, but you won't miss it!

4 slices	Yves Veggie Pepperoni	1/2 tsp	oregano leaves
	1/2" dice	1 tbsp	chopped parsley
3 cups	dry fusili pasta (8 oz)	1/4 cup	green onions, chopped
1 cup	tomato sauce	1/4 cup	olives, chopped
	(recipe page 90 or your	1 cup	carrots, diced
	favorite pasta sauce)	1 cup	cauliflower florets, bite size
6 tbsp	red wine vinegar	1 cup	broccoli florets, bite size
1 tsp	salt	1/2 cup	red bell pepper, 1/2" dice
1/8 tsp	pepper	1/2 cup	green bell pepper,
1/2 tsp	basil leaves		1/2" dice

1. Cook pasta according to directions on package. Drain and
   rinse under cold water. Drain well and transfer to large bowl.
2. Add tomato sauce, vinegar, salt, pepper, basil, oregano,
   parsley, green onions, olives, carrots, cauliflower, broccoli,
   bell peppers and Yves Veggie Pepperoni. Gently mix.
3. If possible, refrigerate for 1 hour. Adjust seasoning, as salad
   may need a little more vinegar after it sits.

MAKES 10 CUPS

NUTRITIONAL ANALYSIS

PER CUP

Calories	92
Protein	4 g
Carbohydrate	16 g
Fat	0.7 g
Dietary fiber	2 g

% CALORIES FROM

Protein	20%
Fat	7%
Carbohydrate	73%

CAESAR SALAD
WITH VEGGIE BACON BITS

Here's a healthy version of a perennial favorite, with 70 percent less fat. Drying the washed lettuce leaves serves two functions: it allows dressing to cling to leaves and it removes water that would otherwise dilute a very flavorful dressing.

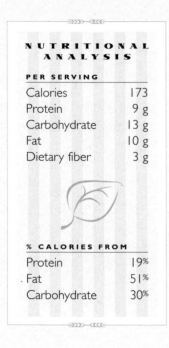

NUTRITIONAL ANALYSIS

PER SERVING

Calories	173
Protein	9 g
Carbohydrate	13 g
Fat	10 g
Dietary fiber	3 g

% CALORIES FROM

Protein	19%
Fat	51%
Carbohydrate	30%

I head	Romaine lettuce (8 cups)	2–3 tbsp	parmesan cheese or grated soy cheese
1½ cups	fat-free or regular croutons	¼ cup	Veggie Bacon Bits (see recipe page 59)
½ cup	Caesar dressing (see recipe next page)		

1. Lay head of Romaine on cutting board and cut lettuce into bite-size pieces, approximately 1" square.
2. Rinse lettuce in cold water and spin or pat dry with clean tea towel.
3. Place leaves in large bowl along with croutons, Caesar dressing, parmesan cheese and Veggie Bacon Bits.
4. Toss until leaves are coated with dressing.

MAKES 4 SERVINGS

CAESAR DRESSING

Caesar Salad was invented in Tijuana in 1924, appropriately by a chef named Caesar Cardini. As in our recipe, the original did not include anchovies. Most Worcestershire sauces list anchovies as an ingredient, however completely plant-based sauces (such as 'Wizard' brand) are also available, often in health food stores.

2 cloves	garlic, minced	2 tsp	lemon juice
3 tbsp	white wine vinegar	I tsp	honey
3 tbsp	grated Parmesan cheese	½ tsp	crushed black pepper
I tbsp	Dijon mustard	½ tsp	salt
2 tsp	minced capers	½ cup	olive oil
2 tsp	Worcestershire sauce	I cup	yogurt

1. In medium bowl, combine garlic, vinegar, cheese, mustard, capers, Worcestershire sauce, lemon juice, honey, pepper and salt. Stir to mix well.
2. In a steady stream, slowly whisk oil into mixture.
3. Gently stir in yogurt. Do not over mix or yogurt will liquefy.

MAKES 2 CUPS DRESSING

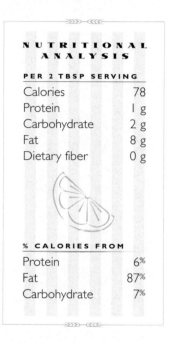

NUTRITIONAL ANALYSIS

PER 2 TBSP SERVING

Calories	78
Protein	I g
Carbohydrate	2 g
Fat	8 g
Dietary fiber	0 g

% CALORIES FROM

Protein	6%
Fat	87%
Carbohydrate	7%

CHEF SALAD
WITH YVES VEGGIE DELI SLICES

Any of Yves Veggie Cuisine slices work well in this salad: Veggie Turkey, Ham, Pepperoni or Deli Slices, so branch out and try some new ones. Similarly, there are many varieties of greens; Romaine, butterhead or red lettuce are crisp, refreshing choices. This salad provides protein, vitamins A, B_{12} (in Yves Slices), C, and calcium. For an even lower fat version, simply skip the cheese.

2 slices	Yves Veggie Deli Slices (or other Yves slices)	2 tbsp	shredded cheddar cheese
2 cups	chopped greens	3	red pepper rings
1/2	egg cut into 2 wedges	2 tbsp	salad dressing of your choice
3	tomato wedges		

1. Cut Yves Deli Slices in half. Place halves on top of each other and cut into thin strips. Set aside.
2. If you have a salad spinner, wash and spin-dry greens. Otherwise, lay lettuce on clean, dry towel to drain water. Chop lettuce into bite-size pieces.
3. On plate, form bed of lettuce.
4. Artistically arrange egg, tomato wedges, cheese, red pepper and Yves Deli Slices on lettuce.
5. Serve with 2 tbsp of your favorite salad dressing.

MAKES 1 SERVING

NUTRITIONAL ANALYSIS

PER SERVING (WITHOUT DRESSING)

Calories	177
Protein	16 g
Carbohydrate	12 g
Fat	8 g
Dietary fiber	4 g

% CALORIES FROM

Protein	35%
Fat	26%
Carbohydrate	39%

PER SERVING (WITHOUT CHEESE, WITHOUT DRESSING)

Calories	117
Protein	13 g
Carbohydrate	12 g
Fat	3 g
Dietary fiber	4 g

% CALORIES FROM

Protein	40%
Fat	22%
Carbohydrate	38%

BALSAMIC VINAIGRETTE

Balsamic vinegar is an Italian specialty derived from the sweet juice of white grapes and made in the province of Modena, using a lengthy aging process. Always used sparingly, it delivers a pleasant mixture of both sweet and tart flavors to cold and hot dishes. In vinaigrette, it offers a deep, rich flavor that enhances salad greens, steamed vegetables, and raw vegetables arranged on a platter.

²/₃ cup	extra virgin olive oil		2 cloves	garlic, minced
¹/₄ cup	lemon juice		1 tsp	salt
2 tbsp	balsamic vinegar		Pinch	pepper

1. In jar with tightly fitting lid, shake together oil, lemon juice, vinegar, garlic, salt and pepper for 30 seconds.
2. Store in closed jar in refrigerator for 3-4 weeks.

MAKES 1 1/4 CUPS

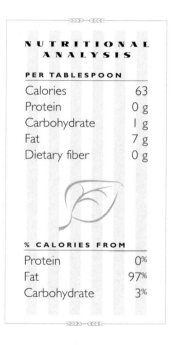

NUTRITIONAL ANALYSIS

PER TABLESPOON

Calories	63
Protein	0 g
Carbohydrate	1 g
Fat	7 g
Dietary fiber	0 g

% CALORIES FROM

Protein	0%
Fat	97%
Carbohydrate	3%

SPINACH SALAD

WITH VEGGIE BACON BITS

Spinach and leafy greens such as kale and collards contain lutein, a relative of vitamin A (beta-carotene). Lutein has been shown to protect the health of our eyes, and to prevent degeneration of the eyes as we age.

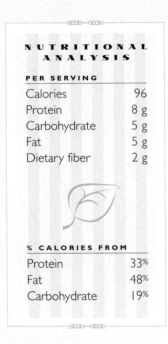

NUTRITIONAL ANALYSIS

PER SERVING

Calories	96
Protein	8 g
Carbohydrate	5 g
Fat	5 g
Dietary fiber	2 g

% CALORIES FROM

Protein	33%
Fat	48%
Carbohydrate	19%

1	bunch spinach (3 cups)	2 tbsp	Veggie Bacon Bits,
1 cup	thinly sliced mushrooms		(see recipe page 59)
1	hard boiled egg, grated	2 tbsp	Creamy Basil Dressing,
1/2 tsp	fresh dill, or 1/8 tsp dried		(see recipe next page)

1. While still in a bunch, cut stems from spinach leaves. Wash leaves thoroughly to remove sand or silt. Spin, shake or pat dry to remove moisture.
2. Tear leaves into bite size pieces, place in large bowl along with mushrooms, egg, dill and bacon bits.
3. Toss, and arrange on 2 salad plates.
4. Pour dressing over top of each serving.

MAKES 2 SERVINGS

NUTRITIONAL NOTE:

In dressed salads, the percentage of calories from fat tends to be high, because oil in the dressing is a concentrated source of calories. At the same time, there are not many calories, nor grams of fat, in the whole salad. Yves Veggie Cuisine's fat free products are important salad ingredients, because they add protein without adding fat.

CREAMY BASIL DRESSING

Freshly cut basil secretes aromatic oils that invite us to taste and enjoy. The creamy ingredients in this recipe carry the flavor of basil well, and impart delightful summer freshness to the greens with which they are served. A tablespoon of regular mayonnaise contains more than 11 grams of fat, whereas a tablespoon of this creamy dressing has only 2.

I cup	yogurt	I tsp	Dijon mustard
¹/₂ cup	light or regular mayonnaise	¹/₄ tsp	salt
2 tbsp	chopped fresh basil	Pinch	pepper
I tbsp	apple cider vinegar		

1. In medium bowl, combine ingredients and mix well.
2. Store in closed jar in refrigerator for up to 3 weeks.

MAKES 1 ¹/₂ CUPS

NUTRITIONAL ANALYSIS

PER TABLESPOON

Calories	23
Protein	0.4 g
Carbohydrate	0.9 g
Fat	2 g
Dietary fiber	0 g

% CALORIES FROM

Protein	7%
Fat	78%
Carbohydrate	15%

CREAMY DILL MAYO

"Dill" may refer either to dill weed, the feathery green leaves of the plant, or to dill seeds. The fresh leaves are our choice for this recipe, as they release the most flavor and aroma. Fresh dill weed is readily available during summer months and can be found year round in many supermarkets. If unavailable, use dry dill weed.

I cup	light or regular mayonnaise	¹/₂ tsp	salt
2 tbsp	apple cider vinegar	Pinch	pepper
2 tbsp	chopped fresh dill		

1. In medium bowl, stir ingredients together.
2. Keep in closed jar, refrigerated, for up to 3 weeks.

MAKES 1 ¹/₄ CUPS

NUTRITIONAL ANALYSIS

PER TABLESPOON

Calories	50
Protein	0 g
Carbohydrate	I g
Fat	5 g
Dietary fiber	0 g

% CALORIES FROM

Protein	0%
Fat	91%
Carbohydrate	9%

TOMATO-BASIL DRESSING

In this light yet flavorful dressing, tomato juice provides body and considerably reduces the amount of oil required. As variations, you may substitute tomato-vegetable juice for tomato juice, and apple cider vinegar for lemon juice. Try different herbs such as oregano or dill, on their own or in combination. If you use dried herbs instead of fresh, use one third the amount specified for fresh herbs.

1 cup	tomato juice	2 tsp	chopped fresh basil
2 tbsp	lemon juice	1 tsp	Dijon mustard
2 tbsp	apple cider vinegar	1/2 tsp	dried tarragon (optional)
2 tbsp	extra-virgin olive oil	Pinch	pepper

1. In jar with lid, combine tomato juice, lemon juice, vinegar, oil, basil, mustard, tarragon (if using), and pepper. Shake for 30 seconds. Store in refrigerator for up to 2 weeks.

MAKES 1 1/4 CUPS

NUTRITIONAL NOTE:
Because there are few calories in this dressing, the percentage calories contributed by the small amount of oil appears large. Also look at the grams of fat per tablespoon. It's low!

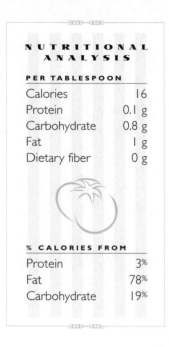

NUTRITIONAL ANALYSIS

PER TABLESPOON

Calories	16
Protein	0.1 g
Carbohydrate	0.8 g
Fat	1 g
Dietary fiber	0 g

% CALORIES FROM

Protein	3%
Fat	78%
Carbohydrate	19%

VEGGIE BACON BITS

WITH YVES CANADIAN VEGGIE BACON

At last! Veggie Bacon Bits with great taste and mouth feel! These delicious morsels are easy to make, using Yves fat-free Canadian Veggie Bacon and a tiny amount of oil. Oil can be cut even further by misting the pan with an oil spray. Store Veggie Bacon Bits in a closed container, refrigerated, for up to 1 month. They can be sprinkled over salads, baked potatoes, tacos, used as a garnish for soups or hot dogs, stirred into omelets and added to the filling in wraps.

1 pkg	Yves Canadian Veggie Bacon	2 tsp	olive oil or spray

1. Cut Yves Veggie Bacon into 1/4" dice.
2. Sauté Yves Veggie Bacon in oil over medium heat, stirring occasionally for 2–3 minutes or until it begins to brown.
3. Place Yves Veggie Bacon in food processor and pulse until it is crumbly and resembles bits.
4. Cool before storing.

MAKES 1 CUP

NUTRITIONAL ANALYSIS

PER TABLESPOON

Calories	20
Protein	3 g
Carbohydrate	0.4 g
Fat	0.6 g
Dietary fiber	0 g

YVES VEGGIE CUISINE

% CALORIES FROM

Protein	66%
Fat	28%
Carbohydrate	6%

SANDWICHES, HOT DOGS & BURGERS

Reuben Sandwich

Hercules Hero

Submarine Sandwich

Traditional Clubhouse Sandwich

Veggie BLT

Sloppy Joes Sandwich

Cheddar Bacon Veggie Burger

Classic Burger Burger

Sautéed Mushroom Bacon Veggie Burger

Veggie Patch Burger

Chicago Style Veggie Hot Dog

Texas Veggie Chili Dog

The Works Veggie Hot Dog

REUBEN SANDWICH & HERCULES HERO

PROTEIN COMPLEMENTATION - AN UPDATE

Have you heard that plant protein is 'incomplete' and needs to be carefully combined with other plant foods to get all the amino acids you need? Here's an update. A best selling book of the 1970s, 'Diet for a Small Planet', encouraged people to include more plant protein in their diets. At the same time, this book fostered the idea (based primarily on animal research) that to meet one's needs, it was necessary to carefully combine protein from different plant foods at meals.

With time, that idea has been corrected to reflect more recent scientific understanding that it is easy to obtain all the protein we need on plant based diets, as long as we get enough calories.

In fact, it is a very good idea to eat a variety from the different food groups over the course of a day, sticking primarily to the healthier foods. Variety brings with it a wealth of the minerals, vitamins and other nutrients we require. But, as for meeting our protein requirements, unless our diets are heavily weighted towards fats and sweets, when we get enough calories, we get enough protein and all essential amino acids without the meticulous protein complementation that was once thought necessary.

REUBEN SANDWICH

Legend has it that the Reuben sandwich was first created in
1914 for one of Charlie Chaplin's leading ladies when she
arrived, very hungry, at the legendary Reuben's Delicatessen in
New York. This delicious sandwich has 12 grams less fat than
a traditional corned beef or ham Reuben, and it is packed with
B vitamins, calcium, iron, zinc and protein, not to mention flavor.
Sauerkraut, Swiss cheese, rye bread, Dijon mustard and Yves
Canadian Veggie Bacon make an outstanding combination.

1 pkg	Yves Canadian Veggie Bacon	6 slices	Swiss cheese
3 tbsp	Dijon mustard	³/₄ cup	sauerkraut
6 slices	rye bread		

1. Steam, sauté or microwave Yves Veggie Bacon until heated
   through.
2. Spread mustard on bread slices and use 3 slices as bottoms
   for sandwiches.
3. Divide Yves Veggie Bacon amongst the 3 sandwiches.
   Quickly place cheese on hot Yves Veggie Bacon so cheese
   melts slightly. If desired, place under broiler for 30 seconds
   to melt cheese completely.
4. Divide sauerkraut equally between sandwiches and top
   with remaining 3 slices of bread.

MAKES 3 SANDWICHES

(See photo page 61)

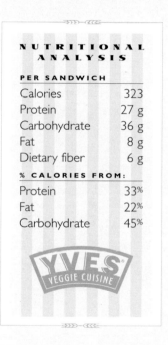

NUTRITIONAL ANALYSIS

PER SANDWICH

Calories	323
Protein	27 g
Carbohydrate	36 g
Fat	8 g
Dietary fiber	6 g

% CALORIES FROM:

Protein	33%
Fat	22%
Carbohydrate	45%

YVES VEGGIE CUISINE

HERCULES HERO
WITH YVES VEGGIE PIZZA PEPPERONI

This sandwich, designed for the Herculean appetite, can be created using 3 slices of Yves Veggie Turkey, Veggie Ham, Veggie Pepperoni or Deli Slices, or with 12 of the smaller Pizza Pepperoni slices. Our Hero is welcome in bag lunches, at home, or for picnics in the park. Chock-full of flavor, color and nutrition, it delivers hefty amounts of protein, calcium, iron and B vitamins.

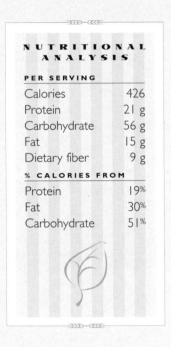

NUTRITIONAL ANALYSIS

PER SERVING

Calories	426
Protein	21 g
Carbohydrate	56 g
Fat	15 g
Dietary fiber	9 g

% CALORIES FROM

Protein	19%
Fat	30%
Carbohydrate	51%

12 slices	Yves Veggie Pizza Pepperoni	2 tbsp	chopped ripe black olives
6" piece	Baguette bread (2 oz), cut lengthwise, or	3 slices	tomato
		5 slices	red onion rings
2 slices	whole wheat bread	2 tbsp	feta cheese
2 tbsp	Dijon mustard (or to taste)	1 leaf	green lettuce

1. Spread mustard on both pieces of bread.
2. Arrange Yves Pizza Pepperoni (or other Yves slices) on one piece of bread.
3. Sprinkle olives on top of Yves Veggie Pepperoni followed by tomato slices, onion, feta, and lettuce. If desired, you may place sandwich under the broiler for 20 seconds to melt the feta cheese before adding the lettuce.
4. Cover with other piece of bread.

MAKES 1 SANDWICH

SUBMARINE SANDWICH

WITH YVES VEGGIE TURKEY, PEPPERONI & DELI SLICES

When feeding a gang, rather than making lots of sandwiches, build a few big subs, then cut them into smaller sections. Supermarkets sell whole wheat and plain submarine buns separately and in bags of 6 or 8. Hoagie buns or French baguettes can also be used to make this scrumptious combination. Eat the entire sub and you'll have about two-thirds of the day's recommended protein intake.

I	submarine bun	2 slices	Yves Veggie Pepperoni
I tbsp	low-fat mayonnaise or	2 slices	Yves Veggie Deli Slices
	Italian dressing	3 slices	tomato
I tsp	prepared mustard	Pinch	salt
2 slices	cheddar cheese	Pinch	pepper
2 slices	Yves Veggie Turkey	¼ cup	shredded lettuce

1. Cut all Yves Veggie Cuisine slices in half or leave whole, depending on width of the bun. Set aside.
2. Cut bun in half lengthwise. Spread mayonnaise on bottom half, mustard on top.
3. Arrange cheese on bottom half, followed by Yves Veggie Turkey, Pepperoni, Deli Slices and tomato slices.
4. Sprinkle salt and pepper; add lettuce and top half of bun.

MAKES 1–2 SERVINGS

NUTRITIONAL ANALYSIS

PER 1/2 SUB:

Calories	341
Protein	21 g
Carbohydrate	43 g
Fat	9 g
Dietary fiber	3 g
% CALORIES FROM	
Protein	25%
Fat	24%
Carbohydrate	51%

TRADITIONAL CLUBHOUSE SANDWICH

WITH YVES VEGGIE TURKEY & BACON

This sandwich is undoubtedly a beloved lunchtime food. It is convenient; an appealing combination of colors, textures and flavors and it is packed with protein, iron and B vitamins. Combining Yves Veggie Turkey and Yves Canadian Veggie Bacon, this 'Triple Decker' is designed for those with hearty appetites.

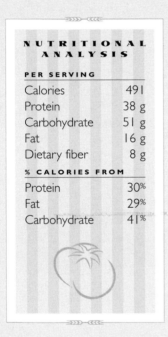

NUTRITIONAL ANALYSIS

PER SERVING

Calories	491
Protein	38 g
Carbohydrate	51 g
Fat	16 g
Dietary fiber	8 g

% CALORIES FROM

Protein	30%
Fat	29%
Carbohydrate	41%

3 slices	Yves Veggie Turkey	1–2	lettuce leaves
3 slices	Yves Canadian Veggie Bacon	4 slices	ripe tomato
½ tsp	olive oil	Pinch	salt
3 slices	whole wheat bread	Pinch	black pepper
2 tbsp	light mayonnaise		

1. Sauté Yves Veggie Bacon over medium heat for 30 seconds on each side.
2. Toast bread and spread mayonnaise on one side of each slice of bread.
3. Place Yves Veggie Turkey and lettuce on bottom piece of toast; cover with second slice of toast.
4. Place Yves Veggie Bacon and tomato on center slice of toast. Sprinkle salt and pepper on tomato and top with remaining piece of toast
5. Cut diagonally into 4 pieces and serve.

MAKES 1 SANDWICH

VEGGIE BLT

WITH YVES CANADIAN VEGGIE BACON

Healthy eating doesn't mean giving up scrumptious combinations like bacon-lettuce-tomato sandwiches! Using Yves fat-free Canadian Veggie Bacon, instead of 4 strips of regular bacon, cuts the fat content of this sandwich in half. Find the best whole grain bread you can, toast it, and get ready for a tasty treat!

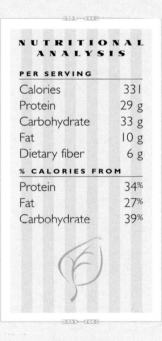

4 slices	Yves Canadian Veggie Bacon	4 slices	ripe tomato
½ tsp	olive oil	Pinch	salt
2 slices	whole wheat bread	Pinch	black pepper
I tbsp	light mayonnaise	I	lettuce leaf

1. Sauté Yves Veggie Bacon in oil over medium heat for 1 minute on each side.
2. Toast bread and spread mayonnaise on inner sides of bread.
3. Place Yves Veggie Bacon and tomato on bottom piece of bread. Sprinkle salt and pepper on top of tomato.
4. Top with lettuce and bread. Cut in half and serve.

MAKES 1 SANDWICH

NUTRITIONAL ANALYSIS

PER SERVING

Calories	331
Protein	29 g
Carbohydrate	33 g
Fat	10 g
Dietary fiber	6 g

% CALORIES FROM

Protein	34%
Fat	27%
Carbohydrate	39%

SLOPPY JOES SANDWICH

WITH YVES VEGGIE GROUND ROUND

The original 'Joe' for whom this dish was named is unknown, however variations on Sloppy Joes recipes date back to the 1940s. This 60-year update has the same great taste as early versions, but there is no cholesterol or saturated fat in Yves version of a Sloppy Joe (without the optional cheddar). A serving provides more than one third of a day's protein requirement, along with plenty of iron and vitamin C. Kids love this recipe; grown-up kids do too!

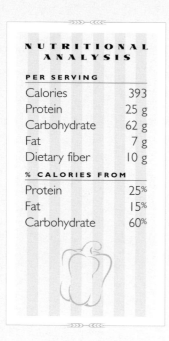

NUTRITIONAL ANALYSIS

PER SERVING

Calories	393
Protein	25 g
Carbohydrate	62 g
Fat	7 g
Dietary fiber	10 g

% CALORIES FROM

Protein	25%
Fat	15%
Carbohydrate	60%

1 pkg	Yves Italian Veggie Ground Round	1 tbsp	Worcestershire sauce (optional)
1–2 tbsp	olive oil	1 tsp	basil leaves
½	medium onion, diced	½ tsp	oregano leaves
½ cup	diced red bell pepper	¼ tsp	salt
½ cup	diced green bell pepper	¼ tsp	coarse black pepper
2	cloves garlic, minced	4	large buns/rolls
2 cups	tomato sauce	½ cup	shredded low-fat cheddar cheese (optional)
⅓ cup	ketchup		

1. Heat oil in large skillet and add onion, peppers and garlic. Sauté for 5–6 minutes.
2. Add tomato sauce, ketchup, Worcestershire sauce (if using), basil, oregano, salt and pepper. Reduce heat to medium and cook, uncovered for about 10 minutes.
3. Add crumbled Yves Italian Ground Round. Stir well and cook 1–2 minutes more.
4. Cut each bun in half and place, open, on serving plates. Top with dollops of Sloppy Joe mixture, and shredded cheese (if using).

MAKES 4 SERVINGS

CHEDDAR BACON VEGGIE BURGER
WITH YVES VEGGIE BACON

In America, the hamburger patty was first known as the 'Hamburg steak', named after the European city and based on a German dish of minced beef. History was made in 1904 at the St. Louis World's Fair, when German immigrants introduced the bun to the patty. Yves Burger Burgers and Yves Canadian Veggie Bacon are a strong and healthful departure from tradition, in that they are fat free, allowing this protein powerhouse to fit within the '30% or less calories from fat' health guidelines, even with cheese and mayo.

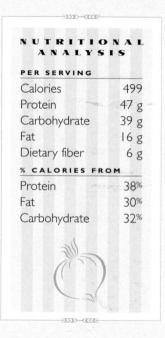

NUTRITIONAL ANALYSIS	
PER SERVING	
Calories	499
Protein	47 g
Carbohydrate	39 g
Fat	16 g
Dietary fiber	6 g
% CALORIES FROM	
Protein	38%
Fat	30%
Carbohydrate	32%

1	Yves Burger Burger	5 slices	thinly sliced red raw onion
2 slices	Yves Canadian Veggie Bacon	2 slices	low fat or regular cheddar cheese
1	hamburger bun		
2 tbsp	low-fat mayonnaise	1/4 cup	shredded lettuce
1 tbsp	chili sauce		

1. Heat Yves Burger Burger over medium heat in nonstick skillet for 2 minutes. Flip over and heat other side for 2 minutes (or microwave according to package directions).
2. Heat Yves Veggie Bacon for 1 minute on each side.
3. Spread both sides of bun with mayonnaise.
4. Place Yves Burger Burger on half of bun.
5. Top with Yves Veggie Bacon.
6. Spread chili sauce over Yves Veggie Bacon.
7. Top with onion, cheese, lettuce and other half of hamburger bun.

MAKES 1 BURGER

CLASSIC BURGER BURGER
MADE WITH YVES BURGER BURGER

Hamburgers are as American, and Canadian, as apple pie. Well over forty billion burgers are consumed in these two countries each year. A classic in its own right, the hamburger is a convenient staple, and a comfort food. Here is a great tasting version, using Yves cholesterol-free, fat-free Burger Burger. Enjoy to your heart's content!

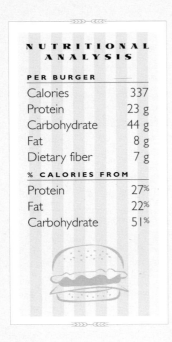

NUTRITIONAL ANALYSIS

PER BURGER

Calories	337
Protein	23 g
Carbohydrate	44 g
Fat	8 g
Dietary fiber	7 g

% CALORIES FROM

Protein	27%
Fat	22%
Carbohydrate	51%

1	Yves Burger Burger	½ tbsp	ketchup
1	hamburger bun	4–5 slices	raw red onion
1–2 tbsp	low-fat mayonnaise	1 slice	tomato
2 tsp	prepared mustard	¼ cup	shredded lettuce leaf
1 tbsp	hamburger relish		

1. Heat Yves Burger Burger over medium heat in skillet for 2 minutes. Flip over and heat other side for 2 minutes.
2. Spread both sides of hamburger bun with mayonnaise.
3. Spread mustard and relish on bottom half of bun; spread ketchup on top half of bun.
4. Place Yves Burger Burger on bottom half of bun and top with onion, tomato, lettuce and top of bun.

MAKES 1 BURGER

CLASSIC BURGER BURGER

FIBER: A BIG BONUS FROM PLANT FOODS

WHAT IS DIETARY FIBER?

It is the roughage from plant foods, the material we don't digest. High fiber foods have few calories – yet they fill you up, so they're great allies if you're watching your waistline. There are two classes of fiber, soluble fiber and insoluble fiber. Soluble fiber gives the gummy quality to oatmeal and thickens the liquid around canned plums and kidney beans. Insoluble fiber gives the crunch to whole wheat bread, carrot sticks and cabbage.

WHY DO WE NEED IT?

Fiber reduces our risk of colon cancer by helping cleanse our systems and regulate bowel function. Insoluble fiber has been called the roto-rooter of the gastro-intestinal tract. It helps food waste move on and out quickly, decreasing our contact with cancer-causing substances. Soluble fiber helps us dispose of unnecessary and unwanted substances. For example it helps lower blood cholesterol, by carrying excess cholesterol that has been excreted into the intestine and right on out of the body.

Dietary fiber helps us to maintain a steady blood glucose level, which is a plus for diabetics, and for non-diabetics too. Soluble fiber forms a gel in the intestine and slows the entry of sugars into the bloodstream.

WHERE DO WE GET IT?

Fiber is not present in foods of animal origin such as meat, fish, poultry or dairy products, however it's found in veggies, whole grains, beans, lentils, fruit – and in many of Yves Veggie Cuisine products.

HOW MUCH DO WE NEED?

A typical North American diet provides only about 14 grams of fiber per day, however we function a lot better on 25 grams or more of fiber daily. A bowl of oatmeal, an apple or a big carrot provides 3 grams of fiber. Look below each recipe in this book, and you'll see how much fiber is in each serving. Yves Fresh Ready-to–Heat entrées are good sources of fiber, too. A serving of the Yves Veggie Cuisine Veggie Country Stew has 12 grams of dietary fiber – and Veggie Chili provides 13 grams – more than half your day's quota! Additional sources are Yves Black Bean and Mushroom Burger (7g/serving) and Yves Garden Vegetable Patty (7g/serving).

SAUTÉED MUSHROOM BACON VEGGIE BURGER

MADE WITH YVES BURGER BURGER & BACON

This burger is destined to be a hit next time you serve it. The combination of Yves Canadian Veggie Bacon, Yves Burger Burger, mushrooms and barbecue sauce is definitely a recipe for more! Whether barbecuing on an outdoor grill or preparing Yves Burgers and Bacon in your kitchen, note that the cooking time needed is just enough to heat the product, as Yves Veggie Cuisine products are precooked.

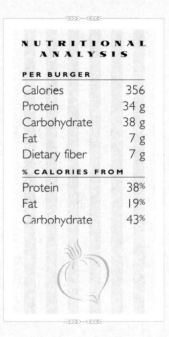

1	Yves Burger Burger	1	hamburger bun
2 slices	Yves Canadian Veggie Bacon	2 tsp	barbecue sauce
1 cup	sliced mushrooms	4 slices	raw red onion
Pinch	salt	1/4 cup	shredded lettuce leaf
1 tbsp	olive oil		

1. In skillet, sauté mushrooms and salt in oil over medium-high heat for 4 minutes or until moisture has evaporated and mushrooms start to brown. Move mushrooms to the side of pan and keep warm.
2. Heat Yves Veggie Bacon in skillet for 1 minute on each side; keep warm.
3. Heat Yves Burger Burger in skillet over medium heat for 2 minutes. Flip over and heat other side for 2 minutes.
4. Meanwhile, spread both sides of bun with barbecue sauce.
5. Place Yves Burger Burger on bottom half of bun, topped with Yves Veggie Bacon.
6. Top with raw onion, mushrooms, lettuce and top of hamburger bun.

MAKES 1 BURGER

NUTRITIONAL ANALYSIS

PER BURGER

Calories	356
Protein	34 g
Carbohydrate	38 g
Fat	7 g
Dietary fiber	7 g

% CALORIES FROM

Protein	38%
Fat	19%
Carbohydrate	43%

VEGGIE PATCH BURGER
MADE WITH YVES GARDEN VEGETABLE PATTY

"Eat Your Veggies" can now be done hamburger-style.
Enjoy this versatile patty with a bakery-fresh bun and your
favorite condiments. Yves Garden Vegetable Patties can also be
cut up and used in tasty dishes such as Sweet and Sour Meatballs,
(page 92), Vegetable Curry on Basmati Rice (page 97) or Gyozas
(page 40).

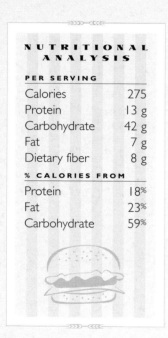

**NUTRITIONAL
ANALYSIS**

PER SERVING

Calories	275
Protein	13 g
Carbohydrate	42 g
Fat	7 g
Dietary fiber	8 g

% CALORIES FROM

Protein	18%
Fat	23%
Carbohydrate	59%

1	Yves Garden Vegetable Patty	1 tbsp	chili sauce
1	hamburger bun	5 slices	thinly sliced red onion
1–2 tbsp	low-fat mayonnaise	1 slice	tomato
		¼ cup	shredded lettuce leaf

1. In skillet, heat Yves Garden Vegetable Patty over medium heat for 2 minutes. Flip over and heat other side for 2 minutes.
2. Meanwhile mix mayonnaise and chili sauce together and spread on both sides of hamburger bun.
3. Place Yves Vegetable Patty on bottom side of bun.
4. Top with onion, tomato, lettuce and top of bun.

MAKES 1 BURGER

CHICAGO STYLE VEGGIE HOT DOG
MADE WITH YVES JUMBO VEGGIE DOG

This tasty hot dog has a nutritional analysis you'd be proud to show your doctor! At the same time, Yves Chicago Style Veggie Hot Dog provides more than one third of the protein needed for the day (typically about 65 g for a man, 50 g for a woman).

1	Yves Jumbo Veggie Dog		1 tbsp	diced tomato
1	hot dog bun		2 tbsp	banana peppers,
1 tbsp	sweet relish			sliced or diced
1 tbsp	prepared mustard		2 tsp	diced onion
1	sliced pickle			

1. Steam or simmer Yves Veggie Dog for 3–5 minutes or until heated through. To heat by microwave, place wiener in microsafe dish, cover with water, loosely cover dish with lid or plastic wrap, and microwave on high power for 2–3 minutes.
2. Slice bun, spread relish on one half of bun and mustard on the other.
3. Place Yves Veggie Dog in bun and arrange pickle, tomato, banana peppers and diced onion on top.

MAKES 1 VEGGIE HOT DOG

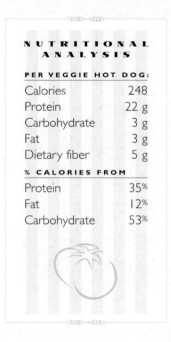

NUTRITIONAL ANALYSIS

PER VEGGIE HOT DOG:

Calories	248
Protein	22 g
Carbohydrate	3 g
Fat	3 g
Dietary fiber	5 g

% CALORIES FROM

Protein	35%
Fat	12%
Carbohydrate	53%

TEXAS VEGGIE CHILI DOG
WITH YVES VEGGIE DOG & CHILI

Here's authentic Texas flavor! We've used Yves Jumbo Veggie Dog, however you may prefer to use Yves Hot and Spicy Jumbo Veggie Dogs, Yves Veggie Chili Dogs, Yves Veggie Wieners or Yves Tofu Wieners.

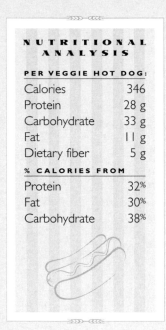

NUTRITIONAL ANALYSIS

PER VEGGIE HOT DOG:

Calories	346
Protein	28 g
Carbohydrate	33 g
Fat	11 g
Dietary fiber	5 g

% CALORIES FROM

Protein	32%
Fat	30%
Carbohydrate	38%

1	Yves Jumbo Veggie Dog	2–3 tsp	low-fat mayonnaise
3 tbsp	Yves Veggie Chili	1 tbsp	prepared mustard
1	hot dog bun	2 tbsp	grated cheddar cheese

1. Steam or simmer Yves Veggie Dog for 3–5 minutes or until heated through. To heat by microwave, place Yves Veggie Dog in microsafe dish, cover with water, loosely cover dish with lid or plastic wrap, and microwave on high power for 2–3 minutes.
2. Meanwhile heat Yves Veggie Chili in small pan or microwave.
3. Slice bun, spread half with mayonnaise and lay Veggie Dog inside.
4. Top Yves Veggie Dog with mustard, chili and cheese.

MAKES 1 VEGGIE HOT DOG

IS YOUR DIET BECOMING MORE PLANT-BASED? MAKE SURE YOU HAVE A SOURCE OF VITAMIN B₁₂

Vitamin B_{12} is required for healthy nerves and for red blood cells to mature properly. In nature, all vitamin B_{12} is produced by tiny single-celled organisms such as bacteria. Though originating from bacteria, this vitamin is present in some animal foods. In order to ensure adequate intakes of this essential nutrient, people on plant-based diets are advised to take a supplement or use a vitamin B_{12}-fortified food. To check if it has been added to a food, look on the ingredient list for vitamin B_{12} (cyanocobalamin).

Many of Yves products are fortified with this important vitamin: Yves Deli Slices, Yves Veggie Ground Round, Yves Italian Ground Round, Yves Veggie Pepperoni, Yves Pizza Pepperoni, Yves Canadian Veggie Bacon, Yves Veggie Wieners, Yves Breakfast Links, and other products listed below.

We need only a tiny amount of vitamin B_{12} in our diets each day – a little more than two micrograms.* You'll get this much vitamin B_{12} in a serving of Yves Veggie Ground Round plus one of Yves Jumbo Veggie Dogs. The recommended intake for vitamin B_{12} is increased by 50 percent during pregnancy. We need only tiny amount of B_{12} – and like the other vitamins, it's essential to life.

YVES VEGGIE CUISINE PRODUCT	SERVING AMOUNT	VITAMIN B¹² (MCG*) IN 1 SERVING	% DV U.S. LABEL	%RDI CANADIAN LABEL
Yves Canadian Veggie Bacon	3 slices (57 g)	1.2 mcg	20%	41%
Yves Deli Slices	4 slices (62 g)	1.2 mcg	20%	61%
Yves Veggie Ground Round	1/3 cup (55 g)	1.4 mcg	25%	71%
Yves Italian Ground Round	1/3 cup (55 g)	1.4 mcg	25%	71%
Yves Veggie Pepperoni	4 slices (62 g)	1.5 mcg	30%	78%
Yves Pizza Pepperoni	16 slices (48 g)	1.2 mcg	20%	60%
Yves Veggie Wieners	1 (46 g)	0.9 mcg	15%	44%
Yves Tofu Wieners	1 (38 g)	0.7 mcg	10%	36%
Yves Veggie Chili Dog	1 (46 g)	0.8 mcg	15%	42%
Yves Hot & Spicy Jumbo Veggie Dog	1 (75 g)	1.4 mcg	25%	69%
Yves Jumbo Veggie Dog	1 (75 g)	1.5 mcg	25%	69%
Yves Veggie Breakfast Links	2 (50 g)	0.9 mcg	15%	44%
Yves Veggie Burger Burger	1 (85g)	1.4 mcg	35%	70%
Yves Veggie Turkey Slices	4 slices (62g)	1.2 mcg	20%	61%
Yves Veggie Ham Slices	4 slices (62g)	1.1 mcg	20%	54%

* MCG MEANS MICROGRAM OR 1/1,000,000 OF A GRAM.

JUMBO VEGGIE DOG

THE WORKS VEGGIE HOT DOG
MADE WITH YVES JUMBO VEGGIE DOG

Condiments, particularly mustard, are an essential part of the hot dog. There are nearly 1,000 varieties of mustard on the market, made from either the mellow yellow seeds, the hot, zesty brown seeds, or a combination. Most of the world's supply of mustard seed is grown on the Canadian plains. In yellow mustards, the distinctive color comes not from the mustard seed, but from the added spice, turmeric. North Americans favor sweet yellow blends and Dijon styles. Each year, more specialty mustards appear on grocery store shelves, so you may want to try a new blend for your next Yves hot dog or burger.

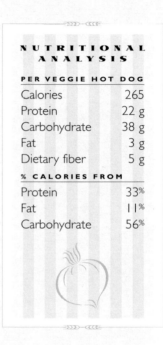

NUTRITIONAL ANALYSIS

PER VEGGIE HOT DOG

Calories	265
Protein	22 g
Carbohydrate	38 g
Fat	3 g
Dietary fiber	5 g

% CALORIES FROM

Protein	33%
Fat	11%
Carbohydrate	56%

1	Yves Jumbo Veggie Dog	1 tbsp	ketchup
1	hot dog bun	2 tbsp	diced onion
2 tbsp	sauerkraut	1 tbsp	prepared mustard
1 tbsp	sweet relish		

1. Steam or simmer Yves Veggie Dog for 3–5 minutes or until heated through. To heat by microwave, place wiener in microsafe dish, cover with water, loosely cover dish with lid or plastic wrap and microwave on high power for 2–3 minutes.
2. Meanwhile, heat sauerkraut in small pan or microwave.
3. Slice bun and spread sauerkraut on bottom half, followed by Yves Veggie Dog.
4. Spread relish on one side of Yves Veggie Dog, ketchup on the other and mustard on top.
5. Sprinkle onion over top of mustard.

MAKES 1 VEGGIE HOT DOG

ENTRÉES

Veggie Pepperoni Farfalle

Spinach Cannelloni

Lasagna al Forno

Spaghetti and Veggie Meatballs

Bolognese Sauce

Tomato Sauce

Veggie Meatballs

Sweet & Sour Veggie Meatballs

Baked Beans with Veggie Wieners

Cabbage Rolls

Hungarian Goulash

Vegetable Curry on Basmati Rice

Stroganoff

Shepherd's Pie

Veggie Pepperoni Pizza

Pizza Dough

Mushroom Gravy

Macaroni and Cheese with Veggie Dogs

Veggie Mexi Mix

VEGGIE PEPPERONI FARFALLE

THE SKINNY ON FATS

There's general agreement among scientific experts that excess dietary fat is damaging to one's health. High fat diets, consumed by so many North Americans, increase the risk of heart disease, hypertension, adult onset diabetes, certain forms of cancer and obesity.

However, not all fat is bad. In fact certain types of fat, known as the essential fatty acids, are actually required for good health. These include omega-3 fatty acids (flaxseed oil is a concentrated source) and omega 6 fatty acids, found in nuts, seeds, whole grains, beans and vegetables. Upon further investigation, we find that it is primarily three types of fat that are linked with health problems: saturated fat, trans fatty acids and cholesterol.

Yves Veggie Cuisine makes it easy for you, with an assortment of products that are fat free and very, very tasty. Yves' products allow you to create an overall diet that provides protein and other essential nutrients, yet provides low or moderate amounts of fat, according to your preference. Many of our recipes give a range in amount of added oils, and are tasty with or without optional ingredients such as sour cream. You can satisfy your taste buds, your appetite and still have a healthful eating pattern.

HIGH-ENERGY FOODS FOR ACTIVE PEOPLE, YOUNG AND OLD

Should all our meals be less than 30 percent calories from fat? Not necessarily. That guideline is great for most adults, most of the time. When the majority of our diet is low in fat, we can afford the occasional splurge. Just watch the portion sizes.

Some lean individuals or high-energy athletes find it a challenge to pack in the calories they need. They fare best by including higher-fat dishes from time to time, eating large portions of energy-giving carbohydrates and by adding healthy snacks between meals.

Growing youngsters, especially those with small appetites, need diets that include some concentrated sources of calories. When it's time for one of those high-energy meals, try the lasagna recipe on page 86, served with a salad and fresh, crusty bread.

VEGGIE PEPPERONI FARFALLE

WITH YVES VEGGIE PEPPERONI

If you haven't cooked with fennel, or the Italian broccoli known as rapini, try them in our elegant pasta dish, shown in the photo on page 81. This warm dish is packed with flavor, an appealing combination of textures, and the antioxidants beta-carotene and vitamin C.

6 slices	Yves Veggie Pepperoni, cut into thin strips	¹/₂	red pepper, julienne
3 cups	dry farfalle or bow tie pasta	¹/₃ cup	de-alcoholized wine or white wine
1¹/₂ tbsp	olive oil	³/₄ cup	vegetable stock
1 cup	onion, sliced lengthwise into thin strips	1¹/₂ cup	broccoli or rapini, cut into florets
1 cup	fennel or zucchini, cut into thin strips		sea salt and freshly ground pepper to taste
³/₄ cup	butternut squash, ¹/₄" dice		freshly grated parmesan or pecorino cheese (optional)
1 tsp	fresh thyme		

<table>
<tr><td colspan="2">NUTRITIONAL ANALYSIS</td></tr>
<tr><td colspan="2">PER SERVING</td></tr>
<tr><td>Calories</td><td>316</td></tr>
<tr><td>Protein</td><td>16 g</td></tr>
<tr><td>Carbohydrate</td><td>44 g</td></tr>
<tr><td>Fat</td><td>8 g</td></tr>
<tr><td>Dietary fiber</td><td>6 g</td></tr>
<tr><td colspan="2">% CALORIES FROM</td></tr>
<tr><td>Protein</td><td>19%</td></tr>
<tr><td>Fat</td><td>22%</td></tr>
<tr><td>Carbohydrate</td><td>59%</td></tr>
</table>

1. Boil pasta in salted water and drain as per package directions.
2. In large saucepan, sauté onion in olive oil over low heat for 2 minutes. Add Yves Veggie Pepperoni and sauté for 3 minutes. Add fennel, squash and sauté another minute.
3. Add thyme and red pepper, increase heat to medium high and cook for 2 minutes. Add wine, bring to a boil and cook 1–2 minutes.
4. Stir in stock, bring to a boil, and add broccoli. Cook until just tender, 2–3 minutes.
5. Mix in pasta and cook 1 minute. Season to taste. Serve with freshly grated parmesan or pecorino cheese, if desired.

MAKES 3 SERVINGS

(See photo page 81)

SPINACH CANNELLONI
WITH YVES VEGGIE GROUND ROUND

Though this recipe requires a little more time, cooking enthusiasts and gourmets amongst you will find the end result to be most enjoyable. Use the sauce on page 90 or your favorite bottled pasta sauce. In this recipe, filling is piped onto a fresh lasagna noodle as an alternative to the familiar cannelloni tube. If you do not have a piping bag, see note on the next page.*

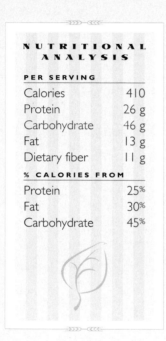

NUTRITIONAL ANALYSIS

PER SERVING

Calories	410
Protein	26 g
Carbohydrate	46 g
Fat	13 g
Dietary fiber	11 g

% CALORIES FROM

Protein	25%
Fat	30%
Carbohydrate	45%

¹/₂ pkg	Yves Veggie Ground Round	¹/₄ tsp	pepper
3 slices	Yves Canadian	1	egg white
	Veggie Bacon, chopped	¹/₂ cup	low-fat ricotta cheese
1	large bunch spinach (4 cups)	2 tbsp	parmesan cheese
¹/₂	medium onion, chopped	2 tbsp	breadcrumbs
2 tbsp	olive oil	2 tbsp	parsley, chopped
2–3	cloves garlic	4	fresh lasagna noodles
¹/₂ tsp	thyme	4 cups	tomato sauce (commercial
¹/₂ tsp	basil		or recipe page 90)
¹/₂ tsp	salt	¹/₂ cup	water
¹/₄ tsp	marjoram		

1. Preheat oven to 350°F.
2. Remove stems from spinach and wash thoroughly to remove dirt and sand. Place in large skillet over medium high heat with ¹/4 cup water and steam for 3–4 minutes or until spinach is wilted.
3. Cool and squeeze out excess moisture with hands. Cut fine and set aside.
4. In skillet, sauté onion in oil over medium heat for 4 minutes or until onion is soft.
5. Add garlic, thyme, basil, salt, marjoram, pepper and sauté for 1 minute.

CONTINUED

CONTINUED

6. Place sautéed seasoning mixture, along with Yves Veggie Ground Round, Yves Veggie Bacon, and egg white into food processor. Puree until mixture is mixed but not fine. Transfer to large bowl.
7. Stir in spinach, ricotta and parmesan cheese, breadcrumbs, parsley and mix thoroughly.
8. Lightly oil 9x12" baking dish. Spread 1/2 cup of tomato sauce on bottom.
9. Place half of the filling mixture into piping bag with a 1" hole.
10. Cut lasagna sheet in half lengthwise and lay on counter.
11. Pipe mixture along bottom edge of sheet.
12. Wet top edge of lasagna sheet with water.
13. Roll sheet towards top and gently press down to seal.
14. Repeat this procedure until mixture is used up. Cut rolls in half and place them in baking dish, seam down.
15. Spread remaining tomato sauce on top, along with water; cover and bake for 1 hour or until noodles are cooked.

MAKES 4 SERVINGS

* **NOTE**: As an alternative to using piping bag, spread the filling 1/4" thick over the surface of the pasta, leaving 1/2" edge at the top to moisten, so the pasta seals when rolled.

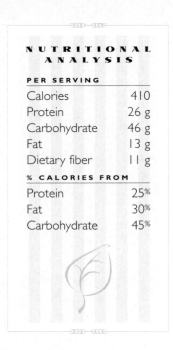

NUTRITIONAL ANALYSIS

PER SERVING

Calories	410
Protein	26 g
Carbohydrate	46 g
Fat	13 g
Dietary fiber	11 g

% CALORIES FROM

Protein	25%
Fat	30%
Carbohydrate	45%

LASAGNA AL FORNO
MADE WITH YVES VEGGIE GROUND ROUND

Lasagna's a favorite, always. The challenge – finding a healthier, lighter version that retains the winning combination of tastes and textures – is accomplished in this recipe. A serving provides well over half the protein and calcium needed for a day, and is an excellent source of iron, zinc and B vitamins. Make a double batch, and keep lasagna in your freezer, to be thawed in the refrigerator and baked when needed.

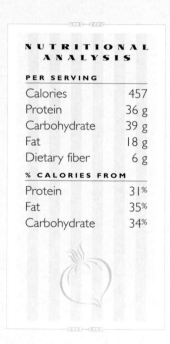

NUTRITIONAL ANALYSIS

PER SERVING

Calories	457
Protein	36 g
Carbohydrate	39 g
Fat	18 g
Dietary fiber	6 g

% CALORIES FROM

Protein	31%
Fat	35%
Carbohydrate	34%

12	lasagna noodles	1/4 cup	frozen spinach, thawed,
1	recipe Bolognese sauce		drained and squeezed dry
	(5 1/2 cups), page 88	1/4 tsp	salt
3/4 cup	onion, chopped	1/4 tsp	black pepper
1 tbsp	olive oil	1/8 tsp	nutmeg
1	clove garlic	2 3/4 cups	grated low fat mozzarella
1 cup	low fat ricotta cheese	1 cup	grated parmesan cheese
1	egg	2 tbsp	chopped parsley

1. Preheat oven to 350°F.
2. Cook noodles according to package directions.
3. In saucepan, sauté onion in oil over medium heat until it starts to brown. Add garlic and sauté for 1 minute. Set aside to cool.
4. Meanwhile, in bowl, combine ricotta cheese, egg, spinach, salt, pepper and nutmeg. Add to onion mixture and stir well.
5. On bottom of lightly oiled 9 x 13" casserole dish, spread 1/2 cup of Bolognese sauce followed by 3 noodles.
6. Spread 1 1/2 cups Bolognese sauce, 1 cup mozzarella and 1/3 cup parmesan cheese. Lay down 3 lasagna noodles, 1 1/2 cups Bolognese sauce, 1 cup mozzarella, 1/3 cup parmesan and 3 noodles.
7. Evenly spread ricotta filling, last 3 noodles and remaining Bolognese sauce. Top with remaining parmesan and mozzarella.
8. Bake for 30–40 minutes or until the liquid on the sides of the dish bubbles. Garnish with chopped parsley and serve.

MAKES 8 SERVINGS

SPAGHETTI & VEGGIE MEATBALLS

MADE WITH YVES VEGGIE GROUND ROUND

The two most commonly asked questions about spaghetti are "How much should I cook per person?" and "When is the pasta cooked?" Here are the answers. First, when you grasp dry spaghetti in your hand, the amount needed per average adult appetite is equivalent in diameter to a 25-cent piece. Second, pasta must be cooked until it slightly resists the bite. Noodles cooked this way are described as *al dente*.

1	recipe Veggie Meatballs (page 91)	4 cups	tomato sauce (commercial or recipe page 90)
1 lb	dry spaghetti noodles		

1. Prepare Veggie Meatballs recipe.
2. Meanwhile, cook noodles according to package directions.
3. Place cooked Veggie Meatballs in small saucepan, cover with tomato sauce, heat for 5 minutes. Serve over cooked noodles.

MAKES 4 SERVINGS

SMART THINKING!

Do you find that you are eating more vegetable protein than you were ten years ago? This choice has been advocated by some very intelligent people, including Pythagorus, Plato, Leonardo da Vinci, Henry David Thoreau, Leo Tolstoy, George Bernard Shaw, Mahatma Gandhi and Albert Einstein.

"Nothing will benefit human health and increase the chances for survival of life on earth as much as the evolution to a vegetarian diet."

ALBERT EINSTEIN
1879–1955

NUTRITIONAL ANALYSIS

PER SERVING	
Calories	700
Protein	39 g
Carbohydrate	122 g
Fat	5 g
Dietary fiber	14 g
% CALORIES FROM	
Protein	22%
Fat	7%
Carbohydrate	71%

YVES
VEGGIE CUISINE

BOLOGNESE SAUCE
WITH YVES VEGGIE GROUND ROUND

Spaghetti with meat sauce, always a favorite, can now be enjoyed using the tremendously versatile Yves Veggie Ground Round. This simple recipe achieves the full, harmonious flavor for which Italian cooking is known. The low-fat sauce is perfect for Lasagna al Forno (page 86), so make extra, and keep a batch in the freezer.

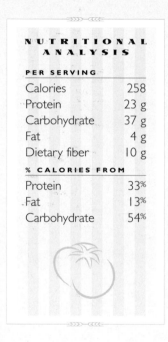

NUTRITIONAL ANALYSIS

PER SERVING

Calories	258
Protein	23 g
Carbohydrate	37 g
Fat	4 g
Dietary fiber	10 g

% CALORIES FROM

Protein	33%
Fat	13%
Carbohydrate	54%

1 pkg	Yves Veggie Ground Round	1 tsp	basil
¹/₂	medium onion, diced	¹/₂ tsp	oregano
1–2 tbsp	olive oil	¹/₂ tsp	salt
2–3	cloves garlic, minced	¹/₄ tsp	black pepper
¹/₂ cup	vegetable stock or red wine	28 oz can	plum or regular tomatoes, puréed
2	bay leaves	¹/₃ cup	tomato paste
1 tbsp	brown sugar		

1. Crumble Yves Veggie Ground Round in medium bowl with fork. Set aside.
2. In saucepan, sauté onion in oil over medium heat 5 minutes or until onion is soft. Add garlic and sauté for 1 minute.
3. Add stock or wine, bay leaves, sugar, basil, oregano, salt, black pepper and cook approximately 4 minutes, to reduce liquid by half.
4. Add tomatoes, tomato paste and stir well. Bring to boil, reduce heat to simmer and cook for 10 to 25 minutes, (longer cooking deepens the flavor).
5. Stir in Yves Veggie Ground Round and heat through.
6. Adjust seasoning and serve over spaghetti noodles.

MAKES 4 SERVINGS

BOLOGNESE SAUCE

TOMATO SAUCE

This recipe is included for those who like to make their own tomato sauce. It can be used as a base for Bolognese Sauce (page 88), Cannelloni (page 84), Cabbage Rolls (page 94), Hawaiian Pizza Squares (page 37) and Veggie Pepperoni Pizza (page 100). Otherwise you may choose among a growing number of delicious gourmet commercial tomato sauces made with mushrooms, roasted garlic, red pepper, herbs, or other seasonings.

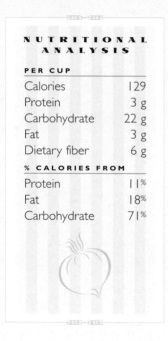

¹/₂	medium onion, diced	1 tsp	basil
1–2 tbsp	olive oil	¹/₂ tsp	oregano
2–3	cloves garlic, minced	¹/₂ tsp	salt
¹/₂ cup	vegetable stock	¹/₄ tsp	black pepper
	or red wine	28 oz can	plum or whole tomatoes,
2	bay leaves		puréed
1 tbsp	brown sugar	¹/₃ cup	tomato paste

1. In saucepan, sauté onion in oil over medium heat for 5 minutes or until onions are soft. Add garlic and sauté for 1 minute.
2. Add stock or wine, bay leaves, sugar, basil, oregano, salt, black pepper and cook for approximately 4 minutes or to reduce liquid by half.
3. Add tomatoes and tomato paste. Bring to boil, reduce heat to simmer and cook for 10 minutes.
4. Adjust seasoning.

MAKES 5¹/₂ CUPS

VEGGIE MEATBALLS

WITH YVES VEGGIE GROUND ROUND

The key to the success of this recipe is developing the gluten.
This can be done with an electric mixer with a paddle, or with
a food processor with a plastic blade, or by vigorous arm action
with a potato masher. You'll get strong arm muscles.

1 pkg	Yves Veggie Ground Round	2 tsp	Worcestershire sauce
1	egg white	1/4 tsp	basil
1/4 cup	wheat gluten	1/4 tsp	thyme
2 tbsp	breadcrumbs	1/4 tsp	oregano
2 tsp	prepared mustard	1/4 tsp	salt

1. Preheat oven to 350°F.
2. In electric mixer using paddle on medium speed, or with food
   processor or potato masher, mix Yves Veggie Ground Round,
   egg white, wheat gluten, breadcrumbs, mustard,
   Worcestershire sauce, basil, thyme, oregano and salt for 2
   minutes or until ingredients are well mixed.
3. Place 2 tbsp of mixture into palm of hand and roll to form
   round ball. Place ball on a lightly oiled baking sheet.
   Continue rolling until mixture is used up.
4. Bake for 20 minutes.

MAKES 12–18 MEATBALLS

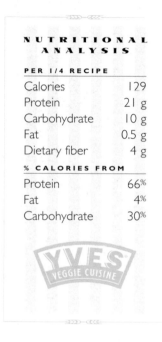

NUTRITIONAL ANALYSIS

PER 1/4 RECIPE

Calories	129
Protein	21 g
Carbohydrate	10 g
Fat	0.5 g
Dietary fiber	4 g

% CALORIES FROM

Protein	66%
Fat	4%
Carbohydrate	30%

SWEET & SOUR VEGGIE MEATBALLS
WITH YVES VEGGIE GROUND ROUND

Although this recipe calls for the Veggie Meatballs, you may substitute Yves Garden Vegetable Patties. Made with two patties, this recipe will feed two hungry adults. To prepare the patties, cut them into 1" square pieces and add to the recipe in step 5, in place of meatballs.

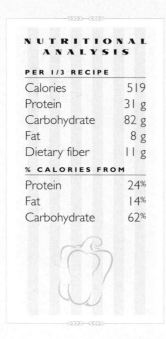

NUTRITIONAL ANALYSIS

PER 1/3 RECIPE

Calories	519
Protein	31 g
Carbohydrate	82 g
Fat	8 g
Dietary fiber	11 g

% CALORIES FROM

Protein	24%
Fat	14%
Carbohydrate	62%

1 recipe	Veggie Meatballs, page 91	**SAUCE**	
1	medium red onion, large dice	1 cup	pineapple juice
3 cloves	garlic, minced	1 1/2 tbsp	cornstarch or arrowroot powder
1 tbsp	peeled minced ginger	1/3 cup	brown sugar
1 cup	red bell pepper, diced	1/4 cup	rice vinegar or white wine vinegar
1 cup	green bell pepper, diced		
1–2 tbsp	olive oil	3 tbsp	soy sauce
1 cup	pineapple chunks	2 tbsp	tomato paste
		1 1/2 tsp	toasted sesame oil

1. Make meatballs using recipe on page 91.
2. While meatballs are baking, sauté onion, garlic, ginger, bell peppers in oil in skillet over medium heat for 5 minutes or until soft.
3. In jar with lid, shake together pineapple juice and cornstarch until dissolved. Add sugar, vinegar, soy sauce, tomato paste, sesame oil and shake to mix sauce.
4. Add sauce to skillet and stir occasionally until thick.
5. Add pineapple chunks, meatballs and heat through.

MAKES 3–4 SERVINGS

BAKED BEANS

Cowboys love baked beans. Kids love baked beans. In fact, they're an all-round favorite. If you have leftovers from this recipe, use some to make Texas Veggie Chili Dogs (page 76).

1 pkg	Yves Veggie Wieners, cut in ½" pieces	1 tbsp	mustard powder
1	medium onion, diced	1 tbsp	cumin powder
1–2 tbsp	olive oil	1 tbsp	salt (or to taste)*
4	cloves garlic, chopped	1½ tsp	thyme
¾ cup	tomato paste	1 tsp	pepper
⅓ cup	molasses	⅛ tsp	clove powder
3 tbsp	red wine vinegar	4½ cups	water
2 tbsp	maple syrup or brown sugar	9½ cups	cooked or canned white beans (3 cups dry beans, cooked)
2 tbsp	Worcestershire sauce		

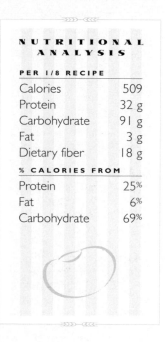

NUTRITIONAL ANALYSIS

PER 1/8 RECIPE

Calories	509
Protein	32 g
Carbohydrate	91 g
Fat	3 g
Dietary fiber	18 g

% CALORIES FROM

Protein	25%
Fat	6%
Carbohydrate	69%

1. Preheat oven to 350°F.
2. In large saucepan, sauté onion over medium heat for 5 minutes or until onions are soft.
3. Add garlic and sauté for 2 minutes.
4. Stir in tomato paste, molasses, vinegar, maple syrup, Worcestershire sauce, mustard, cumin, salt, thyme, pepper, clove powder and water. Stir well to mix.
5. Add cooked beans and transfer to casserole dish.
6. Cover and bake for 1½ hours.
7. Stir in Yves Veggie Wieners and bake for 30 minutes more.

MAKES 6–8 HEARTY SERVINGS

*NOTE: If canned beans that contain salt are used, reduce the amount of salt added.

CABBAGE ROLLS
WITH YVES VEGGIE GROUND ROUND

Here's a highly nutritious version of an old favorite. It's much lower in fat than traditional European cabbage rolls, and this recipe is packed with minerals and vitamins. Yves Veggie Ground Round supplies plenty of protein, iron, zinc, vitamin B_{12} and fiber. But that's not all you'll get from this dinner. Each serving is a source of B vitamins, vitamins A and C, and more calcium than a half-cup of milk!

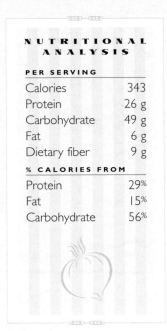

NUTRITIONAL ANALYSIS

PER SERVING

Calories	343
Protein	26 g
Carbohydrate	49 g
Fat	6 g
Dietary fiber	9 g

% CALORIES FROM

Protein	29%
Fat	15%
Carbohydrate	56%

1 pkg	Yves Veggie Ground Round	$^1/_2$ tsp	salt
12	outer leaves of medium green cabbage	$^1/_8$ tsp	pepper
2 cups	cooked rice	$^1/_2$ cup	canned or fresh tomatoes, drained and chopped
1	egg	$^1/_4$ cup	chopped parsley
$^1/_2$	medium onion, diced	$^1/_4$ cup	bread crumbs
3	cloves garlic, minced	2 cups	tomato sauce (recipe page 90 or your favorite pasta sauce)
1–2 tbsp	olive oil		
$^1/_2$ tsp	thyme		

1. Preheat oven to 350°F.
2. With knife, remove core from cabbage and immerse cabbage in large pot of boiling water for 1 minute. Using two forks, gently peel away one leaf at a time until you have removed 12 leaves from the cabbage. Take leaf out of water once it is removed from cabbage.
3. Remove center section of cabbage from water and bring water back to boil. Cook the 12 leaves for 5 minutes, then plunge leaves in cold water to arrest cooking. (Precooking of leaves reduces amount of time needed to bake finished cabbage rolls in oven.)

CONTINUED

CONTINUED

4. Lay leaf on cutting board and remove 2" of rib from base of cabbage leaf. Repeat for all leaves and set aside.

5. In large bowl, mash Yves Veggie Ground Round with fork. Add rice and egg; mix well.

6. In saucepan, sauté onion and garlic in oil over medium heat for 5 minutes or until onions are soft. Stir in thyme, salt, pepper and tomato. Remove from heat; stir in parsley and breadcrumbs.

7. Add to Yves Veggie Ground Round mixture and stir well.

8. Place cabbage leaf on counter or cutting board and place approximately 1/2 cup filling onto center of leaf. Snugly fold all edges towards center of leaf to form a packet or roll. Place roll into lightly oiled casserole dish. Repeat this step using all 12 leaves.

9. Spread tomato sauce over rolls and bake for 30–40 minutes or until leaves are tender.

MAKES 4 SERVINGS, 3 ROLLS EACH

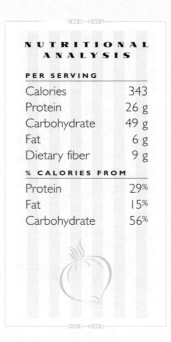

NUTRITIONAL ANALYSIS

PER SERVING

Calories	343
Protein	26 g
Carbohydrate	49 g
Fat	6 g
Dietary fiber	9 g

% CALORIES FROM

Protein	29%
Fat	15%
Carbohydrate	56%

HUNGARIAN GOULASH

WITH YVES BURGER BURGER

The sweet red peppers that are used to make paprika actually originated in Mexico. Over centuries, the plant was taken to the Mediterranean area and eventually to Hungary, where this seasoning contributes flavor and color to many traditional dishes. The peppers used are dried and then ground, creating a lovely deep red powder. Paprika keeps best when air and light are excluded, so use opaque, tightly sealed containers. If your spice jars are clear, keep them in a dark cupboard. Paprika quickly loses its color and aroma, so buy small quantities and discard it if it becomes brown and stale.

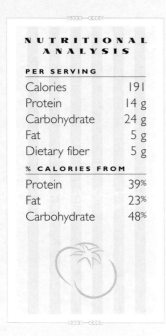

NUTRITIONAL ANALYSIS

PER SERVING

Calories	191
Protein	14 g
Carbohydrate	24 g
Fat	5 g
Dietary fiber	5 g

% CALORIES FROM

Protein	39%
Fat	23%
Carbohydrate	48%

2	Yves Burger Burgers	2 tbsp	all-purpose flour
1/2	medium onion, diced	1 tbsp	paprika
2–3	cloves garlic, minced	1 1/2 cups	vegetable stock
1–2 tbsp	olive oil	1/2 cup	canned tomato, drained and chopped
1/2 tsp	caraway seeds (ground)		
1/2 cup	stock or white wine	1 cup	potatoes, diced

1. Cut both Yves Burger Burger patties into 4 equal strips lengthwise, turn at a 90 degree angle and cut again into 4 equal strips.
2. In saucepan, sauté onion and garlic in oil over medium heat for 5 minutes or until onion is soft.
3. Add caraway seeds, 1/2 cup stock or wine, and cook approximately 4 minutes to reduce liquid by half.
4. Stir in flour, paprika and gradually add stock, stirring constantly. Add tomato, potatoes and Burger Burger. Bring to boil, reduce heat, cover and simmer for 10 minutes or until potatoes are cooked.

MAKES 3 SERVINGS

VEGETABLE CURRY ON BASMATI RICE

WITH YVES GARDEN VEGETABLE PATTIES

Curries are carefully blended combinations of powdered spices that traditionally include cumin, coriander, chili, cloves, cardamom, cinnamon and black pepper. Turmeric gives the mixture its distinctive yellow color. There is no universally accepted recipe, in fact Indian households are likely to have unique blends, ranging from mild to very hot, and with proportions handed down over generations.

2	Yves Garden Vegetable Patties	1/2 tsp	cumin powder
		1/2 cup	coconut milk*
1 cup	raw basmati rice	1 1/2 cups	original or vanilla soymilk
1/4 cup	raisins	1/2 cup	red pepper, diced
1/4 cup	boiling water	1/2 cup	green pepper, diced
1	red onion, large dice	1/2 cup	carrots, diced
1 tbsp	olive oil	1/2 tsp	salt
2 tsp	minced, peeled gingerroot	Pinch	pepper
1–2	cloves garlic, minced	1/4–1/2 tsp	hot sauce (optional)
1 tsp	curry powder		

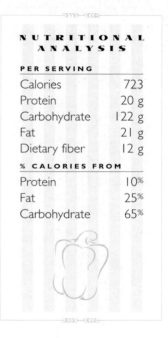

NUTRITIONAL ANALYSIS

PER SERVING

Calories	723
Protein	20 g
Carbohydrate	122 g
Fat	21 g
Dietary fiber	12 g

% CALORIES FROM

Protein	10%
Fat	25%
Carbohydrate	65%

1. Cut Yves Garden Vegetable Patties into 1/2" cubes. Set aside.
2. In bowl, pour water over raisins and soak for 30 minutes.
3. In saucepan, combine rice with 1 1/2 cups water, bring to boil, reduce heat and simmer 20 minutes.
4. In skillet, sauté onion in oil over medium heat for 5 minutes or until onions are soft.
5. Add ginger, garlic and sauté for 1 minute. Add curry, cumin and stir continuously for 2 minutes to avoid scorching the spices.
6. Add coconut milk, soy milk, Yves Garden Vegetable Patties, peppers, carrots, salt, pepper, hot sauce (if using), raisins and soaking water. Bring to boil, reduce heat and simmer 10 minutes or until carrots are cooked. Serve curry over rice.

MAKES 2 HEARTY SERVINGS

*NOTE: Leftover coconut milk may be stored in the freezer.

STROGANOFF

WITH YVES BURGER BURGER

Vegetable stock, which provides a flavorful base for recipes, can be purchased from supermarkets and health food stores as liquid, stock cubes or powder. Stocks vary considerably in salt content. To prevent cold sour cream from curdling when added to hot liquid, a small amount of hot liquid is mixed with sour cream, then mixture is returned to the pan, in a technique called 'tempering'.

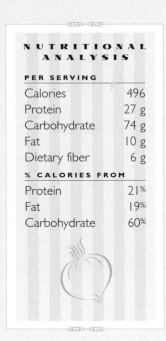

NUTRITIONAL ANALYSIS	
PER SERVING	
Calories	496
Protein	27 g
Carbohydrate	74 g
Fat	10 g
Dietary fiber	6 g
% CALORIES FROM	
Protein	21%
Fat	19%
Carbohydrate	60%

2	Yves Burger Burgers	1 tbsp	prepared mustard
1–2 tbsp	olive oil	1/2 tsp	salt
1/2	medium onion, diced	Pinch	black pepper
2 cups	sliced mushrooms	1 3/4 cups	vegetable stock
1/2 cup	stock or white wine	1/4–1/2 cup	lite or regular sour cream
2 tbsp	all-purpose flour	4 1/2 cups	cooked broad egg noodles
1 tbsp	tomato paste		or rice*

1. Cut Yves Burger Burger patties in half. Crosscut pieces into 1/2" pieces and set aside.
2. In saucepan, sauté onion in oil over medium heat for 5 minutes or until onion is soft. Add mushrooms and sauté 5 minutes or until mushrooms start to brown. Add 1/2 cup stock or wine and reduce liquid by half. Stir in flour, tomato paste, mustard, salt, pepper and cook for 2 minutes, stirring constantly to avoid scorching.
3. Remove from heat for 2 minutes and slowly stir in 1/2 cup of stock. Return to heat and gradually add remaining stock and Yves Burger Burger strips. Cook for 5 minutes.
4. Take about 1/2 cup of hot liquid from pan and add it to sour cream, then stir this mixture into saucepan. Heat through, but do not boil. Serve over noodles or rice.

MAKES 3 SERVINGS

*NOTE: Use 4 cups (200 g) raw noodles or 1 1/2 cups raw rice to make 4 1/2 cups cooked.

SHEPHERD'S PIE

WITH YVES VEGGIE GROUND ROUND

This classic comfort food may stir fond memories from childhood, with the dark, rich, meaty-flavored base, layer of bright yellow corn, and smooth topping of mashed potato. To give a pleasant texture, you may also use a combination of equal amounts of creamed and niblet corn. We suggested the use of white pepper because black pepper gives a speckled appearance to mashed potatoes.

POTATO TOPPING

5	large russet potatoes, peeled (4 lbs purchased)
3–4 tbsp	olive oil
1/2 cup	low fat soy or dairy milk
1/2 tsp	salt
1/2 tsp	white or black pepper

PIE MIXTURE (BASE)

2 pkgs	Yves Veggie Ground Round
2 cups	diced onion
6	cloves garlic, minced
2 cups	chopped celery
1 tbsp	olive oil
2 tbsp	Worcestershire sauce
2 tbsp	soy sauce
2 tsp	tarragon
1/2 tsp	pepper
14 oz can	creamed corn
1/2 tsp	salt
1/4 tsp	paprika

NUTRITIONAL ANALYSIS

PER SERVING

Calories	411
Protein	25 g
Carbohydrate	64 g
Fat	8 g
Dietary fiber	10 g

% CALORIES FROM

Protein	24%
Fat	16%
Carbohydrate	60%

1. Preheat oven to 350°F.
2. Cut each potato into thirds and cook in boiling water until tender.
3. Meanwhile, in skillet, sauté onion, garlic and celery in oil over medium-high heat until soft. Turn off heat, add crumbled Yves Veggie Ground Round, Worcestershire sauce, soy sauce, tarragon, salt, pepper and mix thoroughly.
4. Transfer Yves Veggie Ground Round mixture to sprayed or lightly oiled 9 x 13" casserole dish. Spread mixture and pack evenly.
5. Spread corn over Yves Veggie Ground Round mixture.
6. Drain potatoes, add oil, milk, salt, pepper; mash until fluffy. Spread potato over corn and sprinkle with paprika.
7. Bake for 20 minutes or until heated through.

MAKES 8 SERVINGS

VEGGIE PEPPERONI PIZZA
WITH YVES VEGGIE PEPPERONI

Pizza time is a favorite for kids and adults alike. Children love pizza-building, and this is certainly the easiest way to get them to eat veggies like peppers, mushrooms and tomatoes. More adventurous adults appreciate sliced artichokes, marinated sun dried tomatoes, feta cheese, capers and roasted garlic as toppings. To keep the pizza from getting too chunky, slice all vegetable toppings as thin as possible.

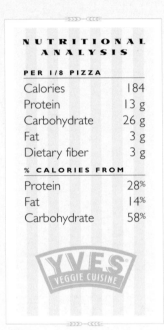

NUTRITIONAL ANALYSIS

PER 1/8 PIZZA

Calories	184
Protein	13 g
Carbohydrate	26 g
Fat	3 g
Dietary fiber	3 g

% CALORIES FROM

Protein	28%
Fat	14%
Carbohydrate	58%

2 pkgs	Yves Veggie Pizza Pepperoni	2 cups	sliced mushrooms
1	Pizza Dough	1 cup	sliced red onion
	(see recipe page 102) or	1 cup	sliced black or green olives
2	12" pre-made pizza shells	2–3 cups	grated mozzarella cheese
3 cups	pizza sauce		parsley (optional)
1	medium green pepper, sliced		

1. Preheat oven to 425°F.
2. Roll out pizza dough and spread onto two 12" round baking trays.
3. Spread sauce evenly over crusts.
4. Distribute Yves Pizza Pepperoni slices evenly over sauce, followed by green pepper, mushrooms, onion and olives.
5. Sprinkle cheese on top.
6. Bake for 25–30 minutes or until the edge and bottoms of crusts are golden brown.
7. Garnish with parsley (if using).

MAKES 2 MEDIUM PIZZAS, 6–8 SLICES EACH

VARIATION: Replace the tomato-based pizza sauce with a thin layer of pesto.

VEGGIE PEPPERONI PIZZA

PIZZA DOUGH

Extra virgin olive oil is worth the extra cost, for use in certain recipes. This oil, from the first pressing of olives, carries a wealth of flavor. As a finishing touch, a thin line of olive oil, drizzled on the edge of the unbaked pizza, results in a crisp, delicious pizza crust. This recipe makes one thick pizza shell for Hawaiian Pizza Squares (page 37) or two thinner 12" crusts, as in the Veggie Pepperoni Pizza (page 100).

2 tbsp	2% milk or soy milk	1 cup	warm water (90°–100°F)
1 tsp	salt	1	package dry active yeast
1 tsp	brown sugar	2³/₄ cups	unbleached flour
1 tbsp	extra virgin olive oil		additional flour for kneading

1. Place milk, salt, sugar, oil and warm water in large stainless steel or glass bowl and mix thoroughly.
2. Sprinkle yeast on top of water mixture and cover bowl tightly with clear kitchen wrap.
3. Fill sink 1/4-full with 100°F water. Place bowl in water and leave for 10 minutes or until yeast mixture is double in size.
4. Slowly stir 1 cup flour into yeast mixture, making a porridge consistency. Gradually add remaining flour and form ball of dough.
5. Knead dough in bowl for 5 minutes.
6. On floured tabletop, further knead dough for 5 minutes. Form round ball and return to bowl. Cover with clean dish towel.
7. Replace water in sink with fresh warm water and place bowl in sink for 30 minutes while dough rises.

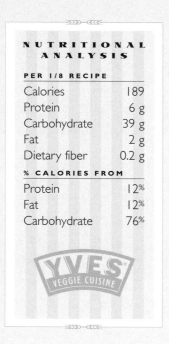

NUTRITIONAL ANALYSIS

PER 1/8 RECIPE

Calories	189
Protein	6 g
Carbohydrate	39 g
Fat	2 g
Dietary fiber	0.2 g

% CALORIES FROM

Protein	12%
Fat	12%
Carbohydrate	76%

MUSHROOM GRAVY

Here's a tasty gravy to use over Veggie Meatballs (page 91), Shepherd's Pie (page 99), or Yves Burger Burgers. Traditional gravy is made using fat drippings from roasted meat. In this cholesterol-free version we use a little olive oil and derive added flavor from mushrooms, vegetable stock, soy sauce, tomato paste, thyme and onion.

4 cups	sliced mushrooms	1 tbsp	tomato paste
1/2	medium onion, diced	3 cups	vegetable stock
1/4 tsp	thyme leaves	1 tbsp	soy sauce
3 tbsp	olive oil	1/8 tsp	pepper
1/4 cup	unbleached white flour		

1. In large saucepan, sauté mushrooms, onions and thyme in oil over medium heat for 5 minutes or until mushrooms start to brown.
2. Stir in flour, tomato paste and cook for 5 minutes, stirring occasionally.
3. Remove pan from heat for 2 minutes to let cool then slowly stir in 1 cup of stock. Return to heat and gradually add remaining stock.
4. Bring to boil, reduce heat and simmer for 10 minutes.
5. Add soy sauce, pepper and season to taste.

MAKES 3 1/2 CUPS

VARIATION: NO-ADDED-OIL GRAVY: Sauté mushrooms, onion and thyme in 3 tbsp vegetable stock. Replace olive oil and flour with 3 tbsp of cornstarch, dissolved in 1/4 cup of cold vegetable stock. Add remaining stock to mushroom-onion mixture and bring to a boil. Slowly mix in the stock with dissolved cornstarch and cook until thickened. Add tomato paste, soy sauce and pepper; use additional soy sauce if needed and season to taste.

NUTRITIONAL ANALYSIS

PER 1/4 CUP

Calories	46
Protein	1 g
Carbohydrate	4 g
Fat	3 g
Dietary fiber	0 g

% CALORIES FROM

Protein	10%
Fat	58%
Carbohydrate	32%

PER 1/4 CUP WITH NO ADDED OIL (VARIATION)

Calories	24
Protein	1 g
Carbohydrate	5 g
Fat	0.4 g
Dietary fiber	0 g

% CALORIES FROM

Protein	21%
Fat	13%
Carbohydrate	66%

MACARONI & CHEESE
WITH YVES VEGGIE DOGS

Pasta's popularity in North America began in the early 1900s with the influx of Italians, their culture and cuisine. For years, American recipes such as "Macaroni and Cheese with Wieners" have been a favorite amoung kids of all ages. It is recommended that when wiener chunks are served to young children, the wieners be cut lengthwise and then into $1/4$" dices, to prevent choking.

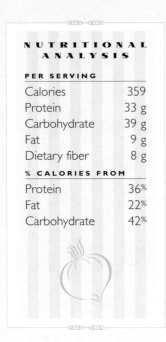

NUTRITIONAL ANALYSIS

PER SERVING

Calories	359
Protein	33 g
Carbohydrate	39 g
Fat	9 g
Dietary fiber	8 g

% CALORIES FROM

Protein	36%
Fat	22%
Carbohydrate	42%

1 pkg	Yves Jumbo Veggie Dogs, Veggie or Tofu Wieners, chopped	2 tbsp	Dijon mustard
		$2^1/_2$ cups	shredded low-fat cheddar cheese
3 cups	dry macaroni	1 tbsp	Worcestershire sauce
1	small onion, minced	$1^1/_2$ tsp	salt
3 tbsp	olive oil	$1/_2$ tsp	nutmeg
3 tbsp	unbleached white flour	$1/_4$ tsp	white pepper
3 cups	1% milk	$1/_4$ cup	chopped fresh parsley

1. Preheat oven to 350° F. Cook macaroni according to package directions. Drain well but do not rinse under water.
2. In saucepan, sauté onion in oil over medium heat for 5 minutes or until onion is soft.
3. Add flour, mix well and cook for 1 minute, stirring to prevent burning.
4. Remove from heat for 2 minutes and gradually add 1 cup milk. Return to heat and slowly add remaining milk.
5. Cook for 5–10 minutes, stirring occasionally, until sauce is smooth and thickened. Add 2 cups cheese, (set $1/2$ cup aside for topping), mustard, Worcestershire sauce, salt, nutmeg, pepper, parsley and stir until cheese is melted.
6. Add pasta, Yves Veggie Dogs, stir and transfer to lightly oiled 8 x 8" baking dish.
7. Top with remaining cheese and bake 30 minutes or until heated through.

MAKES 6 SERVINGS

VEGGIE MEXI MIX

Here's an easy-to-prepare, yet versatile recipe. Use it as a chili entrée, wrap it in tortillas to form burritos, serve it in taco shells, or incorporate it into your favorite baked nacho chip recipe. The recipe below, without the beans, even provides a sauce for Mexican lasagna.

1 pkg	Yves Veggie Ground Round	1 cup	corn, fresh,
1/2	medium onion, diced		canned or frozen
2	cloves garlic, minced	1 tbsp	chili powder
1 tbsp	olive oil	1 tsp	oregano leaves
2 cups	tomato sauce	1/2 tsp	cumin powder
	(recipe page 90 or your	1/2 tsp	basil leaves
	favorite pasta sauce)	1/8 tsp	black pepper
1	14 oz. can kidney beans, drained	2 tbsp	chopped cilantro (optional)

NUTRITIONAL ANALYSIS

PER CUP

Calories	219
Protein	19 g
Carbohydrate	31 g
Fat	3 g
Dietary fiber	9 g

% CALORIES FROM

Protein	33%
Fat	13%
Carbohydrate	54%

1. Transfer Yves Veggie Ground Round to medium bowl and mash with fork. Set aside.
2. In saucepan, sauté onion and garlic in oil over medium heat for 5 minutes or until onions are soft.
3. Add tomato sauce, kidney beans, corn, chili powder, oregano, cumin, basil, pepper and stir.
4. Bring mixture to boil, reduce heat, cover and simmer 5 minutes.
5. Stir in Yves Veggie Ground Round, cilantro (if using) and heat through.

MAKES 6 CUPS

BEVERAGES

Tropic of Chocolate Soy Shake

Cows Go Home Soy Shake

Blue Moon Soy Shake

Super Strawberry Soy Shake

Strawberry Fields Fruit Smoothie

Double Berry Fruit Smoothie

STRAWBERRY FIELDS FRUIT SMOOTHIE

WHAT'S SO SPECIAL ABOUT SOY?

TOP QUALITY PROTEIN

Soy provides your body with top quality protein, and includes all the essential amino acids. In fact, soy protein is equivalent to the protein in meat, milk and eggs.

REDUCED RISK OF HEART DISEASE

Soy protein has been shown to reduce LDL (bad cholesterol) & to decrease risk of heart disease. After extensive research and clinical trials, on October 20, 1999 the United States Food and Drug Administration recognized the importance of soy's cholesterol-lowering effects, and claimed that "Diets low in saturated fat & cholesterol that include 25 grams of soy protein per day may reduce the risk of heart disease."

BENEFICIAL COMPOUNDS SUCH AS ANTIOXIDANTS

Soybeans, and many foods made from soy, contain a number of naturally occurring compounds that are beneficial to our health. These include antioxidants and in particular isoflavones. Antioxidants are the focus of exciting research studies, investigating their actions in protecting cells against damage.

ISOFLAVONES

Soybeans are unique in their content of isoflavones, the most notable being genistein and daidzein. These natural plant components have attracted significant attention from scientific researchers and health professionals. Studies show that isoflavones may provide long-term benefits such as:

- ❏ decreasing the severity of hot flashes for women during menopause;
- ❏ maintaining and even improving lifelong bone health;
- ❏ helping to protect us against certain forms of cancer.

TROPIC OF CHOCOLATE SOY SHAKE

You'll be amazed that a shake can be so easy to make, so low in fat, yet so creamy! With fortified (enriched) soymilk, this shake is a good source of calcium, vitamins B_{12}, D and riboflavin; banana adds potassium and vitamin B_6, and both ingredients provide magnesium.

I cup chocolate soymilk	I	fresh or frozen ripe banana

Place all ingredients into blender and process until smooth. If too thick, add a bit of chocolate soymilk, and blend for 5 seconds.

MAKES 1 1/3 CUPS

NOTE:
Keep frozen bananas on hand for instant use, whenever you need a delicious creamy shake. Simply peel ripe bananas, place them in plastic bags, and store in your freezer.

NUTRITIONAL ANALYSIS

PER SHAKE

Calories	349
Protein	8 g
Carbohydrate	62 g
Fat	5 g
Dietary fiber	3 g

% CALORIES FROM

Protein	10%
Fat	14%
Carbohydrate	76%

COWS GO HOME SOY SHAKE

With only two ingredients, what could be simpler! It's a quick breakfast, an afternoon pick-me-up, and an energy boost for athletes or seniors. Use fortified soymilk to get calcium, vitamins D, B_{12} and all the goodness of soy.

I cup vanilla soymilk	¹/₂	fresh or frozen banana

Place soymilk and banana in blender and process until smooth. If too thick, add a bit of soymilk and blend for 5 seconds.

MAKES 1 1/2 CUPS

NUTRITIONAL ANALYSIS

PER SHAKE

Calories	208
Protein	8 g
Carbohydrate	34 g
Fat	5 g
Dietary fiber	I g

% CALORIES FROM

Protein	15%
Fat	22%
Carbohydrate	63%

BLUE MOON SOY SHAKE

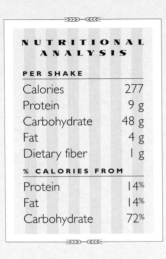

NUTRITIONAL ANALYSIS

PER SHAKE

Calories	277
Protein	9 g
Carbohydrate	48 g
Fat	4 g
Dietary fiber	1 g

% CALORIES FROM

Protein	14%
Fat	14%
Carbohydrate	72%

A botanical name for the cocoa tree means "food for the gods".
This is a heavenly way to enjoy chocolate, along with blueberries
and a touch of yogurt.

¹/₂ cup	chocolate soymilk	¹/₂ cup	fresh or frozen vanilla
¹/₃ cup	fresh or frozen blueberries		yogurt

Place all ingredients into blender and process until smooth.
If too thick, add more chocolate soymilk and blend for 5 seconds.

MAKES 1 CUP

SUPER STRAWBERRY SOY SHAKE

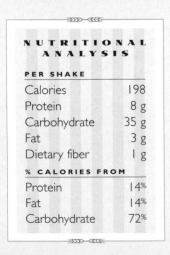

NUTRITIONAL ANALYSIS

PER SHAKE

Calories	198
Protein	8 g
Carbohydrate	35 g
Fat	3 g
Dietary fiber	1 g

% CALORIES FROM

Protein	14%
Fat	14%
Carbohydrate	72%

This yummy shake brings you summer all year long.

¹/₂ cup	vanilla soymilk	¹/₂ cup	fresh or frozen strawberry
¹/₃ cup	fresh or frozen strawberries		yogurt

Place all ingredients into blender and process until smooth.
If too thick, add a bit of vanilla soymilk, and blend for 5 seconds.

MAKES 1 CUP

STRAWBERRY FIELDS FRUIT SMOOTHIE

We've found this to be a favorite with kids. Not only that, it's bursting with vitamin C, so it's good for them!

I cup	orange juice	¹/₃ cup	fresh or frozen strawberries
¹/₂ cup	fresh or frozen vanilla yogurt	¹/₄	fresh or frozen banana

Place all ingredients into blender and process until smooth.
If too thick, add a bit of orange juice, and blend for 5 seconds.

MAKES 1 3/4 CUPS

(See photo page 107)

NUTRITIONAL ANALYSIS

PER SMOOTHIE

Calories	269
Protein	8 g
Carbohydrate	56 g
Fat	2 g
Dietary fiber	2 g

% CALORIES FROM

Protein	11%
Fat	8%
Carbohydrate	81%

DOUBLE BERRY FRUIT SMOOTHIE

This smoothie is delicious!

I cup	apple juice	¹/₂ cup	fresh or frozen strawberry
¹/₄ cup	fresh or frozen raspberries		yogurt
¹/₃ cup	fresh or frozen strawberries		

Place all ingredients into blender and process for 30 seconds or until smooth.

MAKES 1 3/4 CUPS

NUTRITIONAL ANALYSIS

PER SMOOTHIE

Calories	205
Protein	5 g
Carbohydrate	42 g
Fat	2 g
Dietary fiber	3 g

% CALORIES FROM

Protein	9%
Fat	7%
Carbohydrate	84%

GLOSSARY

The following are descriptions of ingredients that you may see listed on nutrition panels of Yves Veggie Cuisine products.

Algin
This gum comes from an edible kelp or seaweed that grows off the coast of California. Algin is used in much the same way as gelatin, to solidify and bind ingredients together.

Beet Root Powder
This natural color derived from beets is used to give some products their reddish color.

Canola Oil
Obtained from the seed of a plant that is a member of the mustard family, much of the world's canola oil is produced in Canada. Canola oil is low in saturated fat, making it a good choice for those who want to watch their blood cholesterol levels.

Carrageenan
Carrageenan is a gum from several seaweed species belonging to the red algae family, found on rocky shores in northern Europe and North America. It is used in a way similar to gelatin, to solidify, or bind ingredients together. It contributes to the texture of Yves Veggie Cuisine products.

Citric Acid
This product of a fermentation process is added to some Yves Veggie Cuisine products in very small quantities to enhance flavor.

Evaporated Cane Juice
This sweetener is made by evaporating moisture from freshly squeezed juice of sun-ripened sugar cane. It contains the sugar sucrose, small amounts of minerals (calcium, iron, magnesium, potassium) and traces of other nutrients.

Gellan Gum
This product of a natural fermentation process adds texture to Yves Veggie Cuisine products.

Guar Gum

This comes from the root of the guar plant, a legume grown in India and parts of the South Western United States. It helps retain moisture in Yves Veggie Cuisine products.

Isolated Soy Protein

An excellent source of protein, containing all nine essential amino acids, isolated soy protein is produced from soybeans by water extraction, resulting in a product with 90% protein content and very little moisture. It is a main ingredient in Yves Veggie Cuisine products, providing nutrition, texture and firmness. The water extraction process promotes retention of soy isoflavones, natural components of soybeans that are valued for a wide range of health benefits.

Konjac Flour

This is a flour and vegetable gum from the Elephant yam, used for centuries in Asia in traditional foods such as noodles.

Locust Bean Gum

Also called carob bean gum, locust bean gum is extracted from seed pods of the carob tree, grown primarily in southern Europe and the Middle East. This gum helps retain moisture and create texture.

Magnesium Chloride

Also known by its Japanese name, nigiri is a naturally occurring salt used in the production of tofu. When added to soymilk, it acts as a coagulant, turning soymilk into tofu curd.

Malt extract

This slightly sweet flavoring comes from sprouted and dried barley.

Natural Flavors/Spices

A variety of natural (rather than synthetic) flavors and spices are used to enhance the delicious taste of Yves products, and in some cases add to the color. Garlic and onion powders provide flavor. Paprika provides a robust reddish color. All our flavors are from vegetable sources. No nitrates or MSG are added to Yves products.

Natural Liquid Smoke
Natural liquid smoke is made from burning hardwoods, such as hickory, with a limited amount of air. The smoke is trapped, and its essence dissolved into purified water.

Nutritional Yeast
This yeast-based supplement, rich in B vitamins, adds nutritional value to Yves Veggie Cuisine products.

Oat Bran
An excellent source of soluble fiber, oat bran comes from the outer layer of oat kernels.

Pea Fiber
Pea fiber, derived from peas, gives texture to products.

Rye Flakes
Rye kernels are heated and then rolled to produce highly nutritious rye flakes.

Rice Starch
Rice starch, the complex carbohydrate that is the main constituent of rice, it gives texture to Yves Veggie Cuisine products.

Soy Protein Isolate: See Isolated Soy Protein

Soy Protein Product: See Textured Soy Protein

Tapioca Starch
Tapioca starch, from the cassava plant, is used for thickening.

Textured Soy Protein/Soy Protein Product
This form of soy protein contains 65%-75% total protein and all essential amino acids. It is unique in that it provides the fibrous texture and 'bite' typical of meat ingredients.

Tofu

Tofu is made from soybeans in a process similar to the production of dairy cheese. Dried soybeans are soaked in water, mashed and cooked, producing soymilk. The pulp is removed and a coagulant, magnesium chloride, is added to the liquid to form curds, which are pressed into creamy white blocks of tofu. Tofu is cholesterol-free, low in saturated fat, and high in protein. It is an excellent source of iron, thiamin, phosphorous, and potassium.

Wheat Germ

Wheat germ is the highly nutritious embryo, or germinating part, of the wheat berry.

Wheat Protein: Wheat Gluten and Textured Wheat Protein

Wheat protein is available in two main forms - wheat gluten and textured wheat protein - and contributes to the wholesomeness and great texture of Yves Veggie Cuisine products. Both have high protein contents and hold water well.

Yeast Extract

Yeast extract are products of a natural fermentation process. They impart a variety of meaty-type 'flavor notes' such as beef, turkey or ham flavors. Once a desirable degree of fermentation is reached, the product is pasteurized and dried into powder.

Xanthan Gum

This product of a natural fermentation process is used to maintain juiciness and add texture to Yves Veggie Cuisine products.

Vitamins and Minerals

Essential for healthy growth and development, vitamins and minerals are added to enhance the nutritional value of Yves Veggie Cuisine products. None are from animal sources. The vitamins used are vitamin B1 (thiamin), vitamin B2 (riboflavin), vitamin B3 (niacin), vitamin B6 (pyridoxine), vitamin B12 (cyanocolabalmin) and pantothenic acid. Minerals used are potassium, iron and zinc. For each product, see ingredient list on label for details.

NOTES